# PASTRIES
# & PIES

~

# Chicken Bobotie

*Perfect for a buffet party, this mild curry dish is set with savoury custard, which makes serving easy. Serve with boiled rice and chutney.*

*Serves 8*

two thick slices white bread

450ml/³/4 pint/1³/4 cups milk

30ml/2 tbsp olive oil

2 medium onions, finely chopped

45ml/3 tbsp medium curry powder

1.25kg/2¹/2lb minced raw chicken

15ml/1 tbsp apricot jam, chutney or caster
    sugar

30ml/2 tbsp wine vinegar or lemon juice

3 small eggs, beaten

50g/2oz/¹/3 cup raisins or sultanas

12 whole almonds

salt and black pepper

3 Mash the bread in the milk and add to the pan with one of the beaten eggs and the raisins.

4 Grease a 1.5 litre/2¹/2 pints/6¹/4 cups shallow ovenproof dish with butter. Spoon in the chicken mixture and level the top. Cover with buttered foil and bake in the oven for 30 minutes.

5 Meanwhile, beat the remaining eggs and milk. Remove the dish from the oven and lower the temperature to 150°C/300°F/Gas 2. Break up the meat using a fork and pour over the egg.

6 Scatter the almonds over and bake, uncovered, for 30 minutes until set and brown.

1 Preheat the oven to 180°C/350°F/Gas 4. Soak the bread in 150ml/¹/4 pint/²/3 cup of the milk. Heat the oil in a frying pan and gently fry the onions until tender, then add the curry powder and cook for a further 2 minutes.

2 Add the minced chicken and brown all over, separating the grains of meat as they brown. Remove from the heat, season with salt and black pepper, add the apricot jam, chutney or caster sugar and the wine vinegar or lemon juice.

# Chicken Bouche

*A spectacular centrepiece, this light pastry case contains a delicious chicken and mushroom filling with a hint of fruit. Ideal served with freshly cooked vegetables.*

*Serves 4*

450g/1lb ready-made puff pastry

beaten egg, to glaze

*For the filling*

15ml/1 tbsp oil

450g/1lb/3 cups minced chicken

25g/1oz/4 tbsp plain flour

150ml/$^1/_4$ pint/$^2/_3$ cup milk

150ml/$^1/_4$ pint/$^2/_3$ cup chicken
   stock

4 spring onions, chopped

25g/1oz/$^1/_4$ cup redcurrants

75g/3oz button mushrooms, sliced

15ml/1 tbsp chopped fresh
   tarragon

salt and black pepper

1 Preheat the oven to 200°C/400°F/Gas 6. Roll half the pastry out on a lightly floured work surface to a 25cm/10in oval. Roll out the remainder to an oval of the same size and draw a smaller 20cm/8in oval in the centre.

2 Brush the edge of the first pastry shape with the beaten egg and place the smaller oval on top. Place on a dampened baking sheet and bake for 30 minutes.

3 For the filling, heat the oil in a large pan. Fry the minced chicken for 5 minutes. Add the flour and cook for a further 1 minute. Stir in the milk and stock and bring to the boil.

4 Add the spring onions, redcurrants and mushrooms. Cook for 20 minutes.

5 Stir in the fresh tarragon and season to taste.

6 Place the pastry bouche on a serving plate, remove the oval centre and spoon in the filling. Place the oval lid on top. Serve with freshly cooked vegetables.

### VARIATION

You can also use shortcrust pastry for this dish and cook as a traditional chicken pie.

# Chicken Liver Stir-fry

*The final sprinkling of lemon, parsley and garlic gives this dish a delightfully fresh flavour and a wonderful aroma.*

## INGREDIENTS

*Serves 4*

500g/1¼ lb chicken livers

75g/3oz/6 tbsp butter

175g/6oz field mushrooms

50g/2oz chanterelle mushrooms

3 cloves garlic, finely chopped

2 shallots, finely chopped

150ml/¼ pint/⅔ cup medium sherry

3 fresh rosemary sprigs

grated rind of 1 lemon

30ml/2 tbsp chopped fresh parsley

salt and black pepper

rosemary sprigs, to garnish

4 thick slices of white toast, to serve

1 Clean and trim the chicken livers to remove any gristle or muscle or discoloured bits.

2 Season the chicken livers generously with salt and ground black pepper, tossing well to coat them all thoroughly.

3 Heat a wok or frying pan and add 15g/½oz/1 tbsp of the butter. When melted, add the livers in batches (melting more butter when necessary but reserving 25g/1oz/2 tbsp for the vegetables) and flash-fry until golden brown. Drain using a slotted spoon and transfer to a plate, then place in a low oven to keep warm.

4 Cut the field mushrooms into thick slices. If large, cut the chanterelles in half.

5 Heat the wok and add the remaining butter. Stir in two-thirds of the chopped garlic and the shallots and stir-fry for 1 minute until golden brown. Stir in the mushrooms and continue to cook for a further 2 minutes.

6 Add the sherry, bring to the boil and simmer for 2–3 minutes until syrupy. Add the rosemary, seasoning and livers to the pan. Stir-fry for 1 minute. Garnish with the rosemary, and sprinkle with a mixture of lemon, parsley and remaining chopped garlic. Serve with slices of toast.

# Curried Chicken and Apricot Pie

*This pie is unusually sweet-sour and very more-ish. Use boneless turkey instead of chicken, if you wish.*

## INGREDIENTS

*Serves 6*

30ml/2 tbsp sunflower oil

1 large onion, chopped

450g/1lb chicken, boned and roughly
    chopped

15ml/1 tbsp curry paste or powder

30ml/2 tbsp apricot or peach chutney

115g/4oz/$^1$/$_2$ cup ready-to-eat dried
    apricots, halved

115g/4oz cooked carrots, sliced

5ml/1 tsp mixed dried herbs

60ml/4 tbsp crème fraîche

350g/12oz ready-made shortcrust pastry

little egg or milk, to glaze

salt and black pepper

3 Roll out the pastry to 2.5cm/1in wider than the pie dish. Cut a strip of pastry from the edge. Damp the rim of the dish, press on the strip, then brush with water and place the sheet of pastry on top, press to seal.

4 Preheat the oven to 190°C/375°F/Gas 5. Trim off any excess pastry and use to make an attractive pattern on the top if you wish. Brush all over with beaten egg or milk and bake for 40 minutes, until crisp and golden.

1 Heat the oil in a large pan and fry the onion and chicken until just colouring. Add the curry paste or powder and fry for another 2 minutes.

2 Add the chutney, apricots, carrots, herbs and crème fraîche to the pan with seasoning. Mix well and then transfer to a deep 900ml–1.2 litre/1$^1$/$_2$–2 pint/4–5 cup pie dish.

# Pan-fried Honey Chicken Drumsticks

*The sweetness of the honey contrasts well with the lemon and soy sauce.*

### INGREDIENTS

*Serves 4*

115g/4oz/$^1$/2 cup clear honey

juice of 1 lemon

30ml/2 tbsp soy sauce

15ml/1 tbsp sesame seeds

2.5ml/$^1$/2 tsp fresh or dried thyme leaves

12 chicken drumsticks

2.5ml/$^1$/2 tsp salt

2.5ml/$^1$/2 tsp pepper

80g/3$^1$/4 oz/$^3$/4 cup flour

45ml/3 tbsp butter or margarine

45ml/3 tbsp vegetable oil

120ml/4fl oz/$^1$/2 cup white wine

120ml/4fl oz/$^1$/2 cup chicken stock

1 In a large bowl, combine the honey, lemon juice, soy sauce, sesame seeds and thyme. Add the chicken drumsticks and mix to coat them well. Leave to marinate in a cool place for 2 hours or more, turning occasionally.

2 Mix the salt, pepper and flour in a shallow bowl. Drain the drumsticks, reserving the marinade. Roll them in the seasoned flour to coat all over.

3 Heat the butter or margarine with the oil in a large frying pan. When hot and sizzling, add the drumsticks. Brown them on all sides. Reduce the heat to medium–low and cook until the chicken is done, 12–15 minutes.

4 Test the drumsticks with a fork; the juices should be clear. Remove the drumsticks to a serving platter and keep hot.

5 Pour off most of the fat from the pan. Add the wine, stock and reserved marinade and stir well to mix in the cooking juices on the bottom of the pan. Bring to the boil and simmer until reduced by half. Check and adjust the seasoning, then spoon the sauce over the drumsticks and serve.

# Chicken Parcels with Herb Butter

*A herb-coated, buttery chicken fillet wrapped up in crisp pastry.*

INGREDIENTS

*Serves 4*

4 chicken breast fillets, skinned

150g/5oz/³/4 cup butter, softened

90ml/6 tbsp chopped mixed fresh herbs, such as thyme, parsley, oregano and rosemary

5ml/1 tsp lemon juice

5 large sheets filo pastry, defrosted if frozen

1 egg, beaten

30ml/2 tbsp grated Parmesan cheese

salt and black pepper

1 Season the chicken fillets and fry in 25g/1oz/2 tbsp of the butter to seal and brown lightly. Allow to cool.

2 Preheat the oven to 190°C/ 375°F/Gas 5. Put the remaining butter, the herbs, lemon juice and seasoning in a food processor and process until smooth. Melt half the herb butter.

3 Take one sheet of filo pastry and brush with herb butter. Cover the rest of the pastry with a damp dish towel. Fold the pastry sheet in half and brush again with butter. Place a chicken fillet about 2.5cm/1in from the top end.

4 Dot the chicken with a quarter of the remaining herb butter. Fold in the sides of the pastry, then roll up to enclose it completely. Place seam-side down on a lightly greased baking sheet. Repeat with the other chicken fillets.

5 Brush the filo parcels with beaten egg. Cut the last sheet of filo into strips, then scrunch and arrange on top. Brush the parcels once again with the egg glaze, then sprinkle with Parmesan cheese. Bake for about 35–40 minutes, until golden brown. Serve hot.

# Chicken Breasts with Tomato-Corn Salsa

*This hot tomato salsa is good with any grilled or barbecued meats.*

## INGREDIENTS

*Serves 4*

4 chicken breast halves, about 175g/6oz
   each, boned and skinned
30ml/2 tbsp fresh lemon juice
30ml/2 tbsp olive oil
10ml/2 tsp ground cumin
10ml/2 tsp dried oregano
15ml/1 tbsp coarse black pepper
salt

*For the salsa*

1 fresh hot green chilli pepper
450g/1lb tomatoes, seeded and chopped
250g/9oz/1$^{1}/_{4}$ cups sweetcorn, freshly
   cooked or thawed frozen
3 spring onions, chopped
15ml/1 tbsp chopped fresh parsley
30ml/2 tbsp chopped fresh coriander
30ml/2 tbsp fresh lemon juice
45ml/3 tbsp olive oil
5ml/1 tsp salt

1 With a meat mallet, pound the chicken breasts between two sheets of clear film until thin.

2 In a shallow dish, combine the lemon juice, oil, cumin, oregano and pepper.

3 Add the chicken and turn to coat. Cover and leave to stand for at least 2 hours, or chill overnight.

4 To make the salsa, char the chilli skin either over a gas flame or under the grill. Leave to cool for 5 minutes. Wearing rubber gloves, carefully rub off the charred skin. For a less hot flavour, discard the seeds.

5 Chop the chilli very finely and place in a bowl. Add the remaining salsa ingredients and mix well.

6 Remove the chicken from the marinade. Season lightly.

7 Heat a ridged grill pan. Add the chicken breasts and cook until browned, about 3 minutes. Turn and cook for 3–4 minutes more. Serve with the chilli salsa.

# Kotopitta

This is based on a Greek chicken pie. Serve hot or cold with a typical Greek salad made from tomatoes, cucumber, onions and feta cheese.

Serves 4

275g/10oz filo pastry

30ml/2 tbsp olive oil

75g/3oz/¹/2 cup chopped toasted
   almonds

30ml/2 tbsp milk

*For the filling*

15ml/1 tbsp olive oil

1 medium onion, finely chopped

1 garlic clove, crushed

450g/1lb cooked chicken, boned

50g/2oz/¹/4 cup feta cheese,
   crumbled

2 eggs, beaten

15ml/1 tbsp chopped fresh parsley

15ml/1 tbsp chopped fresh coriander

15ml/1 tbsp chopped fresh mint

salt and black pepper

1 To make the filling, heat the oil in a large frying pan and cook the chopped onion gently until tender. Add the crushed garlic and cook for a further 2 minutes. Transfer to a bowl.

2 Remove the skin from the chicken and mince or chop finely. Add to the onion with the rest of the filling ingredients. Mix thoroughly and season with salt and freshly ground black pepper.

3 Preheat the oven to 190°C/ 375°F/Gas 5. Have a damp dish towel ready to keep the filo pastry covered at all times. You will need to work fast, as the pastry dries out very quickly when exposed to air. Unravel the pastry and cut the whole batch into a 30cm/12in square.

4 Taking half the sheets (cover the remainder), brush one sheet with a little olive oil, lay it on a well greased 1.35 litre/2¹/4 pint ovenproof dish.

5 Sprinkle with a few almonds. Repeat with the other pastry sheets, overlapping them into the dish. Spoon in the filling and cover the pie in the same way with the rest of the overlapping pastry.

6 Fold in the edges and mark a diamond pattern on the surface with a sharp knife. Brush with milk and sprinkle on any remaining almonds. Bake for 20–30 minutes or until golden.

# Smoked Chicken Pizza

*These ingredients complement each other perfectly and make a really delicious topping.*

INGREDIENTS

*Serves 4*

4 small pizza bases, about 13cm/
    5in diameter
45ml/3 tbsp olive oil
60ml/4 tbsp sun-dried tomato paste
2 yellow peppers, seeded and cut
    into thin strips
175g/6oz sliced smoked chicken
    or turkey, chopped
150g/5oz/1¼ cups mozzarella cheese,
    cubed
30ml/2 tbsp chopped fresh basil
salt and black pepper

1 Preheat the oven to 220°C/
425°F/Gas 7. Place the pizza
bases well apart on two greased
baking sheets.

2 Brush the pizza bases with
15ml/1 tbsp of the oil, then
brush generously with tomato
paste.

3 Stir-fry the peppers in half the
remaining oil for 3–4 minutes.

4 Arrange the chicken and
peppers on top of the sun-
dried tomato paste.

5 Scatter over the mozzarella and
basil. Season to taste with salt
and black pepper.

6 Drizzle over the remaining oil
and bake in the oven for
15–20 minutes until crisp and
golden. Serve immediately.

# Old-fashioned Chicken Pie

The chicken can be roasted and the sauce prepared a day in advance. Leave to cool completely before covering with pastry and baking. Make into four individual pies if you prefer but bake for 10 minutes less.

Serves 4

1.5kg/3–3$^1$/2lb chicken

1 onion, quartered

1 sprig fresh tarragon or rosemary

25g/1oz/2 tbsp butter

115g/4oz/1$^1$/2 cups button mushrooms

30ml/2 tbsp plain flour

300ml/$^1$/2 pint/1$^1$/4 cups chicken stock

115g/4oz cooked ham, diced

30ml/2 tbsp chopped fresh parsley

450g/1lb ready-made puff or flaky pastry

1 egg, beaten

salt and black pepper

1 Preheat the oven to 200°C/ 400°F/Gas 6. Put the chicken into a casserole together with the quartered onion and the herbs. Add 300ml/$^1$/2 pint/1$^1$/4 cups water and season. Cover and roast for about 1$^1$/4 hours or until the chicken is tender.

2 Remove the chicken and strain the liquid into a measuring jug. Cool and remove any fat that settles on the surface. Make up to 300ml/$^1$/2 pint/1$^1$/4 cups with water and reserve for the sauce.

3 Remove the chicken from the bones and cut into large cubes. Melt the butter in a pan, add the mushrooms and cook for 2–3 minutes. Sprinkle in the flour and gradually blend in the stock.

4 Bring to the boil, season to taste and add the ham, chicken and parsley. Turn into a large pie dish and leave to cool.

5 Roll out the pastry on a lightly floured surface to 5cm/2in larger than the pie dish. Cut a narrow strip of pastry to place around the edge of the dish. Dampen with a little water and stick to the rim of the dish. Brush the strip with beaten egg.

6 Lay the pastry loosely over the pie, taking care not to stretch it. Press firmly on to the rim. Using a sharp knife, trim away the excess pastry and knock up the sides to encourage the pastry to rise. Crimp the edge neatly and cut a hole in the centre of the pie. This allows steam to escape during cooking. Decorate with pastry leaves and chill until ready to bake.

7 Brush the pastry with beaten egg (taking care not to glaze over the sides of the pastry). Bake in the oven for 35–45 minutes, until well risen and nicely browned all over.

# Chicken and Shiitake Mushroom Pizza

*The addition of shiitake mushrooms adds an earthy flavour to this colourful pizza, while fresh red chilli gives a hint of spiciness.*

INGREDIENTS

*Serves 3–4*

45ml/3 tbsp olive oil

350g/12oz/3 cups chicken breast fillets, skinned and cut into thin strips

1 bunch spring onions, sliced

1 fresh red chilli, seeded and chopped

1 red pepper, seeded and cut into thin strips

75g/3oz fresh shiitake mushrooms, wiped and sliced

45–60ml/3–4 tbsp chopped fresh coriander

1 pizza base, about 25–30cm/10–12in diameter

15ml/1 tbsp chilli oil

150g/5oz/11/4 cups mozzarella cheese

salt and black pepper

1 Preheat the oven to 220°C/ 425°F/Gas 7. Heat 30ml/2tbsp of the olive oil in a wok or large frying pan. Add the chicken, spring onions, chilli, pepper and mushrooms and stir-fry over a high heat for 2–3 minutes until the chicken is firm but still slightly pink within. Season.

2 Pour off any excess oil, then set aside the chicken mixture until cool.

3 Stir the fresh coriander into the chicken mixture.

4 Brush the pizza base with the chilli oil.

5 Spoon over the chicken mixture and drizzle over the remaining olive oil.

6 Grate the mozzarella and sprinkle over. Bake for 15–20 minutes until crisp and golden. Serve immediately.

# Chicken en Croûte

*Chicken breasts, layered with herbs and orange-flavoured stuffing and wrapped in light puff pastry, make an impressive dish to serve at a dinner party.*

INGREDIENTS

*Serves 8*

450g/1lb packet puff pastry
4 large chicken breasts, boned and skinned
1 egg, beaten

*For the stuffing*

115g/4oz/1 cup leeks, thinly sliced
50g/2oz/$^1$/3 cup streaky bacon, chopped
25g/1oz/2 tbsp butter
115g/4oz/2 cups fresh white breadcrumbs
30ml/2 tbsp chopped fresh herbs, e.g.
    parsley, thyme, marjoram and chives
grated rind of 1 large orange
1 egg, beaten
salt and black pepper

1 To make the stuffing, cook the sliced leeks and bacon in the butter until soft. Put the breadcrumbs into a bowl with the mixed herbs and plenty of seasoning. Add the leeks, bacon and butter with the grated orange rind and bind together with the beaten egg. If the mixture is too dry and crumbly, you can stir in a little orange juice or chicken stock to bring it to a moist consistency.

2 Roll the pastry out to a large rectangle 30 x 40cm/12 x 16in. Trim the edges and reserve for decorating the top.

3 Place the chicken breasts between two pieces of clear film and flatten to a thickness of 5mm/$^1$/4in with a rolling pin. Spread a third of the leek stuffing over the centre of the pastry. Lay two chicken breasts side-by-side on top of the stuffing. Cover the chicken breasts with another third of the stuffing, then repeat with the remaining chicken breasts and the rest of the stuffing.

4 Make a cut diagonally from each corner of the pastry to the chicken. Brush the pastry with beaten egg.

5 Bring up the sides and overlap them slightly. Trim away any excess pastry before folding the ends over like a parcel. Turn over on to a greased baking tray, so that the joins are underneath. Shape neatly and trim any excess pastry.

6 With a sharp knife, lightly criss-cross the pastry into a diamond pattern. Brush with beaten egg and cut leaves from the trimmings to decorate the top. Bake at 200°C/400°F/Gas 6 for 50–60 minutes or until well risen and golden brown on top.

# Oriental Chicken Sandwich

*This filling is also good served in warmed pitta bread, in which case cut the chicken into small cubes before marinating. Grill on skewers and serve warm.*

### INGREDIENTS

*Serves 2*

15ml/1 tbsp soy sauce

5ml/1 tsp clear honey

5ml/1 tsp sesame oil

1 garlic clove, crushed

175g/6oz chicken breast,
    boned and skinned

4 slices white bread

60ml/4 tbsp peanut butter

25g/1oz/2 tbsp beansprouts

25g/1oz red pepper, seeded
    and finely sliced

2 sprigs parsley, to garnish

1 Mix together the soy sauce, honey, sesame oil and garlic. Brush over the chicken breast.

2 Grill the chicken for 3–4 minutes on each side until cooked through, then slice thinly.

3 Spread two slices of the bread with some of the peanut butter.

4 Arrange the slices of chicken on top of the peanut butter.

5 Spread a little more peanut butter over the chicken.

6 Sprinkle over the beansprouts and red pepper and sandwich together with the remaining slices of bread. Cut in half, if desired.

# Chicken Pastitsio

*A traditional Greek pastitsio is a rich, high fat dish made with beef mince, but this lighter version with chicken is just as tasty.*

*Serves 4–6*

450g/1lb lean minced chicken

1 large onion, finely chopped

60ml/4 tbsp tomato purée

250ml/8fl oz/1 cup red wine or stock

5ml/1 tsp ground cinnamon

300g/11oz/2$^1$/2 cups macaroni

300ml/$^1$/2 pint/1$^1$/4 cups milk

25g/1oz/2 tbsp sunflower margarine

25g/1oz/4 tbsp plain flour

5ml/1 tsp grated nutmeg

2 tomatoes, sliced

60ml/4 tbsp wholemeal breadcrumbs

salt and black pepper

green salad, to serve

1 Preheat the oven to 220°C/ 425°F/Gas 7. Fry the chicken and onion in a non-stick pan without fat, stirring until lightly browned.

2 Stir in the tomato purée, red wine or stock and cinnamon. Season, then cover and simmer for 5 minutes, stirring from time to time. Remove from the heat.

3 Cook the macaroni in plenty of boiling, salted water until just tender, then drain.

4 Layer the macaroni with the meat mixture in a wide ovenproof dish.

5 Place the milk, margarine and flour in a saucepan and whisk over a moderate heat until thickened and smooth. Add the nutmeg, and season to taste.

6 Pour the sauce evenly over the pasta and meat layers. Arrange the tomato slices on top and sprinkle lines of wholemeal bread-crumbs over the surface.

7 Bake for 30–35 minutes, or until golden brown and bubbling. Serve hot with a fresh green salad.

# Chicken and Curry Mayonnaise Sandwich

*A very useful and appetizing way of using leftover pieces of chicken.*

*Serves 2*

4 slices Granary bread

25g/1oz/2 tbsp softened butter

115g/4oz cooked chicken, sliced

45ml/3 tbsp Curry Mayonnaise

1 bunch watercress, trimmed

1 Spread the bread with butter and arrange the chicken over two of the slices.

2 Spread the Curry Mayonnaise over the chicken slices.

3 Arrange a few sprigs of watercress on top, cover with the remaining bread, press lightly together and cut in half.

### CURRY MAYONNAISE

*Makes about 150ml/5fl oz/²/₃ cup*

120ml/4fl oz/¹/₂ cup mayonnaise

10ml/2 tsp concentrated curry sauce

2.5ml/¹/₂ tsp lemon juice

10ml/2 tsp sieved apricot jam

Mix all the ingredients together thoroughly and chill until needed.

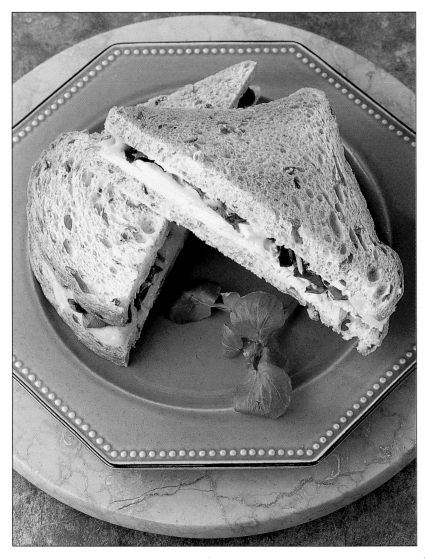

# Chicken and Game Pie

*A rich filling of chicken and dark meat, spiced with ginger.*

## INGREDIENTS

*Serves 4*

450g/1lb boneless chicken and game meat
   (plus the carcasses and bones)

1 small onion, halved

2 bay leaves

2 carrots, halved

a few black peppercorns

15ml/1 tbsp oil

75g/3oz streaky bacon pieces, rinded and
   chopped

15ml/1 tbsp plain flour

45ml/3 tbsp sweet sherry or Madeira

10ml/2 tsp ground ginger

grated rind and juice of $^1/_2$ orange

350g/12oz ready-made puff pastry

beaten egg or milk, to glaze

salt and black pepper

1 Place the carcasses and bones in a pan, with any giblets and half the onion, the bay leaves, carrots and black peppercorns. Cover with water and bring to the boil. Simmer until reduced to about 300ml/$^1/_2$ pint/1$^1/_4$ cups, then strain the stock, ready to use.

2 Cut the chicken and game meat into even-size pieces. Chop, then fry the remaining onion in the oil until softened. Then add the bacon and meat and fry quickly to seal. Sprinkle on the flour and stir until beginning to brown. Gradually add the stock, stirring as it thickens, then add the sherry or Madeira, ginger, orange rind and juice, and seasoning. Simmer for 20 minutes.

3 Transfer to a 900ml/1$^1/_2$ pints/ 3$^3/_4$ cups pie dish and allow to cool slightly. Use a pie funnel to help hold up the pastry.

4 Preheat the oven to 220°C/425°F/Gas 7. Roll out the pastry to 2.5cm/1in larger than the dish. Cut off a 1cm/$^1/_2$in strip all round. Dampen the rim of the dish and press on the strip of pastry. Dampen again and then lift the pastry carefully over the pie, sealing the edges well at the rim. Trim off the excess pastry, use to decorate the top, then brush the pie with egg or milk.

5 Bake for 15 minutes, then reduce the oven temperature to 190°C/375°F/Gas 5, for a further 25–30 minutes.

# Risotto with Chicken

*This is a complete meal cooked conveniently all in one pan.*

INGREDIENTS

*Serves 4*

2 tablespoons olive oil

8oz/225g chicken breast, skinned, boned
and cut into 2.5cm/1in cubes

1 onion, finely chopped

1 garlic clove, finely chopped

1.5ml/$^1/_4$ tsp saffron strands

50g/2oz/$^1/_2$ cup Parma ham, cut
into thin strips

450g/1lb/2 cups risotto rice,
preferably Arborio

120ml/4fl oz/$^1/_2$ cup dry white wine

1.75 litres/3 pints/7$^1/_2$ cups simmering
chicken stock

25g/1oz/2 tbsp butter (optional)

25g/1oz/$^1/_3$ cup freshly grated Parmesan
cheese, plus more to serve

salt and pepper

1 Heat the oil in a wide heavy-based pan over moderately high heat. Add the chicken cubes and cook, stirring, until they start to turn white.

2 Reduce the heat to low. Add the onion, garlic, saffron and Parma ham. Cook, stirring, until the onion is soft. Stir in the risotto rice and mix well. Sauté for 1–2 minutes, stirring constantly.

3 Add the wine and bring to the boil. Simmer gently until almost all the wine is absorbed.

4 Add the simmering stock, a ladleful at a time, and cook until the rice is just tender and the risotto creamy.

5 Add the butter, if using, and Parmesan cheese and stir in well. Season with salt and pepper to taste. Serve the risotto hot, sprinkled with more Parmesan.

# Chicken and Stilton Pies

These individual chicken and Stilton pies are wrapped in a crisp, shortcrust pastry and shaped into pasties. They are great for lunch, served hot or cold.

## INGREDIENTS

*Makes 4*

350g/12oz/3 cups self-raising flour
2.5ml/$^1$/$_2$ tsp salt
75g/3oz/6 tbsp lard
75g/3oz/6 tbsp butter
60–75ml/4–5 tbsp cold water
beaten egg, to glaze

*For the filling*

450g/1lb chicken thighs, boned and
   skinned
25g/1oz/$^1$/$_4$ cup chopped walnuts
25g/1oz spring onions, sliced
50g/2oz/$^1$/$_2$ cup Stilton, crumbled
25g/1oz celery, finely chopped
2.5ml/$^1$/$_2$ tsp dried thyme
salt and black pepper

1 Preheat the oven to 200°C/ 400°F/Gas 6. Mix the flour and salt in a bowl. Rub in the lard and butter with your fingers until the mixture resembles fine bread-crumbs. Using a knife to cut and stir, mix in the cold water to form a stiff, pliable dough.

2 Turn out on to a work surface and knead lightly until smooth. Divide into four and roll out each piece to a thickness of 5mm/$^1$/$_4$in. Cut into a 20cm/8in circle.

3 Remove any fat from the chicken thighs and cut into small cubes. Mix with the chopped walnuts, spring onions, Stilton, celery, thyme and seasoning and divide the filling equally among the four pastry circles.

4 Brush the edge of the pastry with beaten egg and fold over, pinching and crimping the edges together well. Place on a greased baking sheet and bake in the oven for about 45 minutes, or until golden brown.

# Stuffed Chicken Breasts with Cream Sauce

*Chicken breasts filled with a leek and lime-flavoured stuffing and served in a cream sauce.*

## INGREDIENTS

*Serves 4*

4 large chicken breasts,
    boned and skinned

50g/2oz/4 tbsp butter

3 large leeks, white and pale green
    parts only, thinly sliced

5ml/1 tsp grated lime zest

250ml/8fl oz/1 cup chicken stock or half
    stock and half dry white wine

120ml/4fl oz/$^1$/$_2$ cup whipping or
    double cream

15ml/1 tbsp lime juice

salt and pepper

1 Cut horizontally into the thickest part of each breast to make a deep, wide pocket. Take care not to cut all the way through. Set the chicken breasts aside.

2 Melt half the butter in a large heavy frying pan over low heat. Add the leeks and lime zest and cook, stirring occasionally, for 15–20 minutes or until the leeks are very soft but not coloured.

3 Turn the leeks into a bowl and season to taste with salt and pepper. Leave to cool. Wash and dry the frying pan.

4 Divide the leeks among the chicken breasts, packing the pockets full. Secure the openings with wooden cocktail sticks.

5 Melt the remaining butter in the frying pan over moderately high heat. Add the stuffed breasts and brown lightly on both sides.

6 Add the stock and bring to the boil. Cover and simmer for about 10 minutes or until the chicken is cooked through. Carefully turn the breasts over halfway through the cooking.

7 With a slotted spatula, remove the breasts from the pan and keep warm. Boil the cooking liquid until it is reduced by half.

8 Stir the cream into the cooking liquid and boil until reduced by about half again. Stir in the lime juice and season to taste.

9 Remove the cocktail sticks from the breasts. Cut each breast on the diagonal into 1cm/$^1$/$_2$ in slices, pour the sauce over them and serve.

### VARIATION

For Onion-stuffed Chicken Breasts, use 2 sweet onions, halved and thinly sliced, instead of leeks.

# ONE POT
# MEALS

# Stir-fried Chicken with Mange-touts

*Juicy chicken stir-fried with mange-touts, cashews and water chestnuts.*

## INGREDIENTS

*Serves 4*

30ml/2 tbsp sesame oil

90ml/6 tbsp lemon juice

1 garlic clove, crushed

1cm/$^1$/2 in piece fresh root ginger,
    peeled and grated

5ml/1 tsp clear honey

450g/1lb chicken breast fillets,
    cut into strips

115g/4oz mange-touts, trimmed

30ml/2 tbsp groundnut oil

50g/2oz/$^1$/2 cup cashew nuts

6 spring onions, cut into strips

225g/8oz can water chestnuts,
    drained and thinly sliced

salt

saffron rice, to serve

1 Mix together the sesame oil, lemon juice, garlic, ginger and honey in a shallow non-metallic dish. Add the chicken and mix well. Cover and leave to marinate for at least 3–4 hours.

2 Blanch the mange-touts in boiling salted water for 1 minute. Drain and refresh under cold running water.

3 Drain the chicken strips and reserve the marinade. Heat the groundnut oil in a wok or large frying pan, add the cashew nuts and stir-fry for about 1–2 minutes until golden brown. Remove the cashew nuts from the wok or frying pan using a slotted spoon and set aside.

4 Add the chicken and stir-fry for 3–4 minutes, until golden brown. Add the spring onions, mange-touts, water chestnuts and the reserved marinade. Cook for a few minutes, until the chicken is tender and the sauce is bubbling and hot. Stir in the cashew nuts and serve with saffron rice.

# Risotto

*An Italian dish made with short grain arborio rice which gives a creamy consistency to this easy one-pan recipe.*

INGREDIENTS

*Serves 4*

15ml/1 tbsp oil

175g/6oz/1 cup Arborio rice

1 onion, chopped

225g/8oz/2 cups minced chicken

600ml/1 pint/2$^1$/2 cups chicken stock

1 red pepper, seeded and chopped

1 yellow pepper, seeded and
  chopped

75g/3oz/$^3$/4 cup frozen green beans

115g/4oz/1$^1$/2 cups chestnut
  mushrooms, sliced

15ml/1 tbsp chopped fresh parsley

salt and black pepper

fresh parsley, to garnish

3 Pour in the stock and bring to the boil.

4 Stir in the peppers and reduce the heat. Cook for 10 minutes.

5 Add the green beans and mushrooms and cook for a further 10 minutes.

6 Stir in the fresh parsley and season well to taste. Cook for 10 minutes or until the liquid has been absorbed. Serve garnished with fresh parsley.

1 Heat the oil in a large frying pan. Add the rice and cook for 2 minutes until transparent.

2 Add the onion and minced chicken. Cook for 5 minutes, stirring occasionally.

# Poussins with Grapes in Vermouth

*A rather special dish which is ideal to serve when entertaining.*

INGREDIENTS

*Serves 4*

4 oven-ready poussins, about
   450g/1lb each
50g/2oz/4 tbsp butter, softened
2 shallots, chopped
60ml/4 tbsp chopped fresh parsley
225g/8oz white grapes, preferably
   muscatel, halved and seeded
150ml/¼ pint/⅔ cup white vermouth
5ml/1 tsp cornflour
60ml/4 tbsp double cream
30ml/2 tbsp pine nuts, toasted
salt and black pepper
watercress sprigs, to garnish

1 Preheat the oven to 200°C/
400°F/Gas 6. Spread the
softened butter all over the
poussins and put a hazelnut-sized
piece in the cavity of each bird.

2 Mix together the shallots and
parsley and place a quarter of
the mixture inside each poussin.
Put the poussins side by side in a
large roasting tin and roast for
40–50 minutes, or until the juices
run clear when the thickest part of
the flesh is pierced with a skewer.
Put the poussins on to a warm
serving dish, cover and keep warm.

3 Skim off most of the fat from
the roasting tin, then add the
grapes and vermouth. Place the tin
directly over a low flame for a few
minutes to warm and slightly
soften the grapes.

4 Lift the grapes out of the tin
using a slotted spoon and
scatter them around the poussins.
Keep covered. Stir the cornflour
into the cream, then add to the pan
juices. Cook gently for a few
minutes, stirring, until the sauce
has thickened. Adjust seasoning.

5 Pour the sauce around the
poussins. Sprinkle with the
toasted pine nuts and garnish with
watercress sprigs.

# Nasi Goreng

*This dish is originally from Thailand, but can easily be adapted by adding any cooked ingredients you have to hand. Crispy prawn crackers make an ideal accompaniment.*

## INGREDIENTS

*Serves 4*

225g/8oz/1 cup long grain rice

2 eggs

30ml/2 tbsp vegetable oil

1 green chilli

2 spring onions, roughly chopped

2 cloves garlic, crushed

225g/8oz cooked chicken

225g/8oz cooked prawns

45ml/3 tbsp dark soy sauce

prawn crackers, to serve

1 Rinse the rice and then cook for 10–12 minutes in 475ml/16fl oz/2 cups water in a pan with a tight-fitting lid. When cooked, refresh under cold water.

2 Lightly beat the eggs. Heat 15ml/1 tbsp of oil in a small frying pan and swirl in the beaten egg. When cooked on one side, flip over and cook on the other side. Remove from the pan and leave to cool. Cut the omelette into strips.

3 Carefully remove the seeds from the chilli and chop finely, wearing rubber gloves to protect your hands if necessary. Place the spring onions, chilli and garlic in a blender or food processor and blend to a paste.

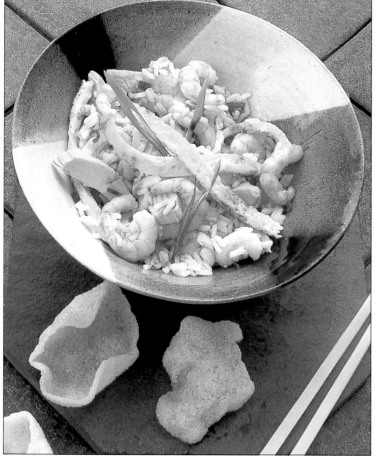

4 Heat the wok, and then add the remaining oil. When the oil is hot, add the chilli paste and stir-fry for 1 minute.

5 Stir the chicken and prawns into the chilli paste.

6 Add the rice and stir-fry for 3–4 minutes. Stir in the soy sauce and serve with prawn crackers.

# Roast Chicken with Celeriac

*Chicken with a stuffing of celeriac, bacon, onion and herbs.*

*Serves 4*

1.6kg/3$^{1}/_{2}$lb chicken

15g/$^{1}/_{2}$oz/1 tbsp butter

*For the stuffing*

450g/1lb celeriac, chopped

25g/1oz/2 tbsp butter

3 slices bacon, chopped

1 onion, finely chopped

leaves from 1 thyme sprig, chopped

leaves from 1 small tarragon
   sprig, chopped

30ml/2 tbsp chopped fresh parsley

75g/3oz/1$^{1}/_{2}$ cups fresh brown
   breadcrumbs

dash of Worcestershire sauce

1 egg

salt and pepper

1 To make the stuffing, cook the celeriac in boiling water until tender. Drain well and chop finely.

2 Heat the butter in a saucepan, then gently cook the bacon and onion until the onion is soft. Stir the celeriac and herbs into the pan and cook, stirring occasionally, for 2–3 minutes. Meanwhile, preheat the oven to 200°C/400°F/Gas 6.

3 Remove the pan from the heat and stir in the fresh bread-crumbs, Worcestershire sauce, seasoning and sufficient egg to bind.

4 Place the stuffing in the neck end of the chicken. Season the bird's skin, then rub with the butter. Roast the chicken, basting occasionally with the juices, for 1$^{1}/_{4}$–1$^{1}/_{2}$ hours, until the juices run clear when the thickest part of the leg is pierced. Rest for 10 minutes in a warm place before carving.

# Chicken and Rice Vermicelli

*This delicious dish makes a filling meal. Take care when frying vermicelli as it has a tendency to spit when added to hot oil.*

INGREDIENTS

*Serves 4*

120ml/4fl oz/$^1$/2 cup vegetable oil

225g/8oz rice vermicelli

150g/5oz French beans, topped, tailed and halved lengthways

1 onion, finely chopped

2 chicken breasts, about 175g/6oz each, boned, skinned and cut into strips

5ml/1 tsp chilli powder

225g/8oz cooked prawns

45ml/3 tbsp dark soy sauce

45ml/3 tbsp white wine vinegar

10ml/2 tsp caster sugar

fresh coriander sprigs, to garnish

1 Heat a wok or frying pan, then add 60ml/4 tbsp of the oil. Break up the vermicelli into 7.5cm/3in lengths. When the oil is hot, fry the vermicelli in batches. Remove from the heat and keep warm.

2 Heat the remaining oil, then add the French beans, chopped onion and chicken and stir-fry together for 3 minutes, until the chicken strips are cooked.

3 Sprinkle in the chilli powder. Stir in the cooked prawns, soy sauce, vinegar and sugar, and stir-fry for 2 minutes.

4 Serve the chicken, prawns and vegetables on the fried vermicelli, garnished with sprigs of fresh coriander.

# Traditional Roast Chicken

*Serve with bacon rolls, chipolata sausages, gravy and stuffing balls.*

INGREDIENTS

*Serves 4*

1.75kg/4lb chicken

streaky bacon rashers

25g/1oz/2 tbsp butter

salt and black pepper

*Prune and nut stuffing*

25g/1oz/2 tbsp butter

50g/2oz/$^1$/$_2$ cup chopped stoned
    prunes

50g/2oz/$^1$/$_2$ cup chopped walnuts

50g/2oz/1 cup fresh breadcrumbs

1 egg, beaten

15ml/1 tbsp chopped fresh parsley

15ml/1 tbsp chopped fresh chives

30ml/2 tbsp sherry or Port

*For the gravy*

30ml/2 tbsp plain flour

300ml/$^1$/$_2$ pint/1$^1$/$_4$ cups chicken stock

1 Preheat the oven to 190°C/
375°F/Gas 5. Mix all the
stuffing ingredients together in a
bowl and season well.

2 Stuff the neck end of the
chicken quite loosely, allowing
room for the breadcrumbs to swell
during cooking. (Any remaining
stuffing can be shaped into balls
and fried to accompany the roast.)

3 Tuck the neck skin under the
bird to secure the stuffing and
hold in place with the wing tips or
sew with strong thread or fine
string.

4 Place in a roasting tin and
cover the breast with the bacon
rashers. Spread with the remaining
butter, cover loosely with foil and
roast for about 1$^1$/$_2$ hours. Baste
with the juices in the roasting tin
3 or 4 times during cooking.

5 Remove any trussing string and
transfer to a serving plate,
cover with foil and leave to stand
while making the gravy. (This
standing time allows the flesh to
relax and makes carving easier.)

6 Spoon off the fat from the
juices in the roasting tin. Blend
the flour into the juices and cook
gently until golden brown. Add the
stock, bring to the boil, stirring until
thickened. Adjust the seasoning
and strain into a jug to serve.

# Chinese Special Fried Rice

*Cooked white rice fried with a selection of other ingredients is a staple Chinese dish. This recipe combines a mixture of chicken, shrimps and vegetables with fried rice.*

### INGREDIENTS

*Serves 4*

175g/6oz/1 cup long grain white rice

45ml/3 tbsp groundnut oil

1 garlic clove, crushed

4 spring onions, finely chopped

115g/4oz/1 cup diced cooked chicken

115g/4oz/1 cup cooked peeled shrimps
    (rinsed if canned)

50g/2oz/$\frac{1}{2}$ cup frozen peas

1 egg, beaten with a pinch of salt

50g/2oz/1 cup shredded lettuce

30ml/2 tbsp light soy sauce

pinch of caster sugar

salt and black pepper

15ml/1 tbsp chopped roasted cashew nuts,
    to garnish

1 Rinse the long grain rice in two to three changes of warm water to wash away some of the starch. Drain well.

2 Put the rice in a saucepan and add 15ml/1 tbsp of the oil and 350ml/12fl oz/1$\frac{1}{2}$ cups of water. Cover and bring to the boil, stir once, then cover and simmer for 12–15 minutes, until nearly all the water has been absorbed. Turn off the heat and leave covered for 10 minutes. Fluff up with a fork and leave to cool.

3 Heat the remaining oil in a wok or frying pan, add the garlic and spring onions and stir-fry for 30 seconds.

4 Add the chicken, shrimps and peas and stir-fry for 1–2 minutes, then add the cooked rice and stir-fry for a further 2 minutes. Pour in the egg and stir-fry until just set. Stir in the lettuce, soy sauce, sugar and seasoning.

5 Transfer to a warmed serving bowl, sprinkle with the chopped roasted cashew nuts and serve immediately.

# Chicken Roll

*The roll can be prepared and cooked the day before and will freeze well too. Remove from the fridge about an hour before serving.*

*Serves 8*

2kg/4¹/₂lb chicken

*For the stuffing*

1 medium onion, finely chopped
50g/2oz/4 tbsp melted butter
350g/12oz/2 cups lean minced pork
115g/4oz streaky bacon, chopped
15ml/1 tbsp chopped fresh parsley
10ml/2 tsp chopped fresh thyme
115g/4oz/2 cups fresh white breadcrumbs
30ml/2 tbsp sherry
1 large egg, beaten
25g/1oz/¹/₄ cup shelled pistachio nuts
25g/1oz/¹/₄ cup stoned black olives
    (about 12)
salt and black pepper

1 To make the stuffing, cook the chopped onion gently in 25g/1oz/2 tbsp of the butter until soft. Turn into a bowl and cool. Add the remaining ingredients, mix thoroughly and season with salt and black pepper.

2 To bone the chicken, use a small, sharp knife to remove the wing tips. Turn the chicken on to its breast and cut a line down the backbone.

3 Cut the meat away from the carcass, scraping the bones clean. Carefully cut through the sinew around the leg and wing joints and scrape down the bones to free them. Remove the carcass, taking care not to cut through the skin along the breastbone.

4 To stuff the chicken, lay it flat, skin side down and flatten as much as possible. Shape the stuffing down the centre of the chicken and fold in the sides.

5 Sew the meat neatly together, using a needle and dark thread. Tie with fine string into a roll.

6 Preheat the oven to 180°C/ 350°F/Gas 4. Put the roll, join underneath, on a rack in a roasting tin and brush with the remaining butter. Cook, uncovered, for about 1¹/₄ hours. Baste with the juices during cooking. Leave to cool. Remove the string and thread. Wrap in foil and chill until needed.

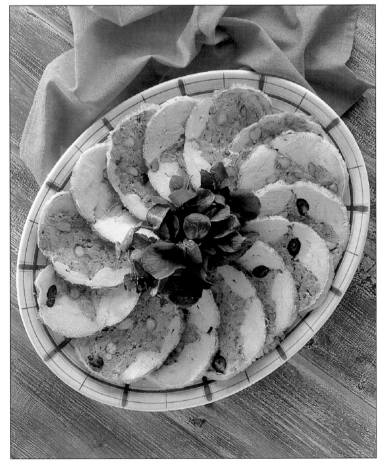

# Chicken Teriyaki

Boiled rice is the ideal accompaniment to this Japanese-style dish.

Serves 4

450g/1lb chicken breasts, boned and
    skinned
orange segments and mustard and cress,
    to garnish

*For the marinade*
5ml/1 tsp sugar
15ml/1 tbsp rice wine
15ml/1 tbsp dry sherry
30ml/2 tbsp dark soy sauce
rind of 1 orange, grated

1 Finely slice the chicken breasts to give thin strips. Mix all the marinade ingredients together in a bowl.

2 Place the chicken in a bowl, pour over the marinade and leave to marinate for 15 minutes.

3 Heat a wok or large frying pan, add the chicken and marinade and stir-fry for 4–5 minutes. Serve the chicken garnished with orange segments and mustard and cress.

## COOK'S TIP

Make sure the marinade is brought to the boil and cooked for 4–5 minutes, because it has been in contact with raw chicken.

# Chicken and Tomato Hot-pot

*Versatile minced chicken is perfect for family meals. Here, it's turned into tasty meatballs.*

### INGREDIENTS

*Serves 4*

25g/1oz white bread, crust removed

30ml/2 tbsp milk

1 garlic clove, crushed

2.5ml/$^1$/2 tsp caraway seeds

225g/8oz/2 cups minced chicken

1 egg white

350ml/12fl oz/1$^1$/2 cups chicken stock

400g/14oz can plum tomatoes

15ml/1 tbsp tomato purée

90g/3$^1$/2oz/$^1$/2 cup easy-cook rice

salt and black pepper

15ml/1 tbsp chopped fresh basil,
    to garnish

carrot and courgette ribbons, to serve

4 Put the chicken stock, tomatoes and tomato purée into a large, heavy-based saucepan and bring to the boil.

5 Add the rice, stir and cook briskly for about 5 minutes. Turn the heat down to a simmer.

6 Meanwhile, shape the chicken mixture into 16 small balls. Carefully drop them into the tomato stock and simmer for a further 8–10 minutes, or until the chicken balls and rice are cooked. Garnish with the basil, and serve with carrot and courgette ribbons.

1 Cut the bread into small cubes and put into a mixing bowl. Sprinkle over the milk and leave to soak for 5 minutes.

2 Add the garlic clove, caraway seeds, chicken, salt and freshly ground black pepper to the bread. Mix together well.

3 Whisk the egg white until stiff, then fold, half at a time, into the chicken mixture. Chill for 10 minutes in the fridge.

# Thai Fried Noodles

*Pork, chicken and fish stir-fried with noodles and lime juice.*

*Serves 4*

225g/8oz thread egg noodles
60ml/4 tbsp vegetable oil
2 garlic cloves, finely chopped
175g/6oz pork tenderloin, sliced into thin
    strips
1 chicken breast (about 175g/6oz), boned,
    skinned and sliced into thin strips
115g/4oz/1 cup cooked peeled shrimps
    (rinsed if canned)
45ml/3 tbsp lime or lemon juice
45ml/3 tbsp oriental fish sauce
30ml/2 tbsp soft light brown sugar
2 eggs, beaten
$1/2$ red chilli, seeded and finely chopped
50g/2oz/$1/4$ cup beansprouts
60ml/4 tbsp roasted peanuts, chopped
3 spring onions, cut into 5cm/2in lengths
    and shredded
45ml/3 tbsp chopped fresh coriander

1 Place the noodles in a large pan of boiling water and leave to stand for about 5 minutes.

2 Meanwhile, heat 45ml/3 tbsp of the oil in a wok or large frying pan, add the garlic and cook for 30 seconds. Add the pork and chicken and stir-fry on a high heat until lightly browned, then add the shrimps and stir-fry for 2 minutes.

3 Add the lime or lemon juice, fish sauce and sugar and stir-fry until the sugar has dissolved.

4 Drain the noodles and add to the pan with the remaining 15ml/1 tbsp oil. Toss all the ingredients together.

5 Pour on the beaten eggs. Stir-fry until almost set, then add the chilli and beansprouts. Divide the peanuts, spring onions and coriander leaves into two and add half to the pan. Stir-fry for 2 minutes, then tip on to a serving platter. Sprinkle on the remaining peanuts, spring onions and coriander and serve at once.

# Blackened Chicken Breasts

*Chicken breasts with a seasoned coating of herbs and spices.*

INGREDIENTS

*Serves 6*

6 medium chicken breasts,
    boned and skinned
75g/3oz/6 tbsp butter or margarine
5ml/1 tsp garlic purée
60ml/4 tbsp finely grated onion
5ml/1 tsp cayenne
10ml/2 tsp sweet paprika
7.5ml/1$^{1}/_{2}$ tsp salt
2.5ml/$^{1}/_{2}$ tsp white pepper
5ml/1 tsp black pepper
1.5ml/$^{1}/_{4}$ tsp ground cumin
5ml/1 tsp dried thyme leaves

1 Slice each chicken breast piece in half horizontally. Flatten them down slightly with the heel of the hand.

2 Melt the butter or margarine in a small saucepan together with the garlic purée.

3 Combine all the remaining ingredients in a shallow bowl and stir well. Brush the chicken pieces on both sides with melted butter or margarine, then sprinkle evenly with the seasoned mixture.

4 Heat a large heavy frying pan over high heat until a drop of water sprinkled on the surface sizzles. This will take 5–8 minutes.

5 Drizzle 5ml/1 tsp of melted butter on each chicken piece. Place them in the pan in an even layer, 2 or 3 at a time. Cook until the underside begins to blacken, 2–3 minutes. Turn over and cook 2–3 minutes more. Serve hot.

# Burgundy Chicken

*A dinner-party classic, perfect with a good bottle of red wine.*

INGREDIENTS

*Serves 4*

60ml/4 tbsp plain flour

1.5kg/3lb chicken, cut into 8 joints

15ml/1 tbsp olive oil

65g/2$^{1}$/2oz/5 tbsp butter

20 baby onions

75g/3oz piece streaky bacon without rind, diced

about 20 button mushrooms

75cl bottle red Burgundy wine

bouquet garni

3 garlic cloves

5ml/1 tsp soft light brown sugar

salt and black pepper

15ml/1 tbsp chopped fresh parsley and croûtons, to garnish

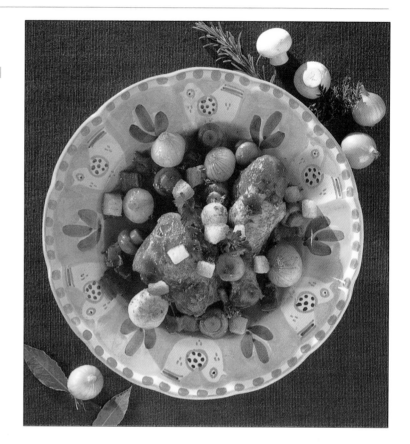

1 Place 45ml/3 tbsp of the flour and the seasoning in a large plastic bag and shake each chicken joint in it until lightly coated. Heat the oil and 50g/2oz/4 tbsp of the butter in a large flameproof casserole. Add the onions and bacon and sauté for 3–4 minutes, until the onions have browned lightly. Add the mushrooms and fry for 2 minutes. Remove with a slotted spoon into a bowl and reserve.

2 Add the chicken pieces to the hot oil and cook until browned on all sides, about 5–6 minutes. Pour on the Burgundy wine, add the bouquet garni, garlic, soft light brown sugar and seasoning.

3 Bring to the boil, cover and simmer for 1 hour, stirring occasionally.

4 Return the reserved onions, bacon and mushrooms to the casserole, cover and cook for a further 30 minutes.

5 Lift out the cooked chicken, vegetables and bacon with a draining spoon and arrange on a warmed dish. Remove the bouquet garni and boil the liquid rapidly for 2 minutes to reduce slightly. Cream the remaining butter and flour together and whisk in tea-spoonfuls of the mixture until thickened slightly. Pour over the chicken and garnish with parsley and croûtons.

# Oven "Fried" Chicken

*The chicken in this dish is not fried but baked until crisp in the oven.*

*Serves 4*

4 large chicken pieces

50g/2oz/$^1$/2 cup flour

2.5ml/$^1$/2 tsp salt

1.5ml/$^1$/4 tsp pepper

1 egg

30ml/2 tbsp water

30ml/2 tbsp chopped mixed fresh herbs, such as parsley, basil and thyme

65g/2$^1$/2 oz/1 cup dry breadcrumbs

25g/1oz/$^1$/3 cup freshly grated Parmesan cheese

lemon wedges, for serving

1 Preheat the oven to 200°C/ 400°F/Gas 6.

2 Rinse the chicken in cold water. Pat dry with kitchen paper.

3 Combine the flour, salt and pepper on a plate and stir with a fork to mix. Coat the chicken pieces on all sides with the flour and shake off the excess.

4 Sprinkle a little water on to the chicken pieces, and coat again lightly with the seasoned flour.

5 Beat the egg with the water in a shallow dish. Stir in the herbs. Dip the chicken pieces into the egg mixture, turning them over to coat them thoroughly.

6 Combine the breadcrumbs and grated Parmesan cheese on a plate. Roll the chicken pieces in the crumbs, patting with your fingers to help them to adhere.

7 Place the chicken pieces in a greased shallow pan, large enough to hold them in one layer. Bake until thoroughly cooked and golden brown, 20–30 minutes. To check that they are cooked, prick with a fork; the juices that run out should be clear, not pink. Serve hot, with lemon wedges.

# Apricot and Chicken Casserole

*A mild curry and fruity chicken dish served with almond rice. Makes a good winter meal.*

INGREDIENTS

*Serves 4*

15ml/1 tbsp oil

8 chicken thighs, boned and skinned

1 medium onion, finely chopped

5ml/1 tsp medium curry powder

30ml/2 tbsp plain flour

450ml/$^3$/4 pint/1$^7$/8 cups chicken
   stock

juice of 1 large orange

8 dried apricots, halved

15ml/1 tbsp sultanas

salt and black pepper

*For the almond rice*

225g/8oz/2 cups cooked long grain rice

15g/$^1$/2oz/1 tbsp butter

50g/2oz/$^1$/2 cup toasted, flaked almonds

3 Add the apricots and sultanas, cover with a lid and cook gently for an hour, or until tender, in the preheated oven. Adjust the seasoning to taste.

4 To make the almond rice, reheat the pre-cooked rice with the butter and season to taste. Stir in the toasted almonds just before serving.

1 Preheat the oven to 190°C/ 375°F/Gas 5. Heat the oil in a large frying pan. Cut the chicken into cubes and brown quickly all over in the oil. Add the chopped onion and cook gently until soft and lightly browned.

2 Transfer the chicken and onion to a large flameproof casserole and sprinkle in the curry powder and cook again for a few minutes. Add the flour and blend in the stock and orange juice. Bring to the boil and season with salt and freshly ground black pepper.

# Chicken Kiev

*Cut through the crispy-coated chicken to reveal a creamy filling with just a hint of garlic.*

### INGREDIENTS

*Serves 4*

4 large chicken breasts, boned and
   skinned
15ml/1 tbsp lemon juice
115g/4oz/$^1/_2$ cup ricotta cheese
1 garlic clove, crushed
30ml/2 tbsp chopped fresh parsley
1.5ml/$^1/_4$ tsp freshly grated nutmeg
30ml/2 tbsp plain flour
pinch of cayenne pepper
1.5ml/$^1/_4$ tsp salt
115g/4oz/2 cups fresh white breadcrumbs
2 egg whites, lightly beaten
creamed potatoes, French beans and
   grilled tomatoes, to serve

1 Preheat the oven to 200°C/400°F/Gas 6. Place the chicken breasts between two sheets of clear film and gently beat with a rolling pin until flattened. Sprinkle with the lemon juice.

2 Mix the ricotta cheese with the garlic, 15ml/1 tbsp of the chopped parsley and the nutmeg. Shape into four 5cm/2in long rolls.

3 Put one portion of the cheese and herb mixture in the centre of each chicken breast and fold the meat over, tucking in the edges to enclose the filling completely.

4 Secure the chicken with cocktail sticks pushed through the centre of each. Mix together the flour, cayenne pepper and salt and use to dust the chicken.

5 Mix together the breadcrumbs and remaining parsley. Dip the chicken into the egg whites, then coat with the breadcrumbs. Chill for 30 minutes in the fridge, then dip into the egg white and breadcrumbs for a second time.

6 Put the chicken on a non-stick baking sheet. Bake in the preheated oven for 25 minutes or until the coating is golden brown and the chicken completely cooked. Remove the cocktail sticks and serve with creamed potatoes, French beans and grilled tomatoes.

# Chicken in Creamed Horseradish

*The piquant flavour of horseradish sauce gives this quick dish a sophisticated taste. Use half the quantity if using fresh horseradish.*

INGREDIENTS

*Serves 4*

30ml/2 tbsp olive oil

4 chicken pieces

25g/1oz/2 tbsp butter

25g/1oz/2 tbsp plain flour

450ml/$^3$/4 pint/1$^7$/8 cups chicken stock

30ml/2 tbsp creamed horseradish
  sauce

salt and black pepper

15ml/1 tbsp chopped fresh parsley

mashed potatoes and tender French
  beans, to serve

1 Heat the oil in a large flameproof casserole and gently brown the chicken joints on both sides over a medium heat. Remove the chicken from the casserole and keep warm.

2 Wipe out the casserole, melt the butter, stir in the flour and blend in the stock gradually. Bring to the boil, stirring all the time.

3 Add the horseradish sauce and season with salt and freshly ground black pepper. Return the chicken to the casserole, cover and simmer for 30–40 minutes or until the chicken is tender.

4 Transfer to a serving dish and sprinkle with fresh parsley. Serve with mashed potatoes and French beans, if desired.

# Mediterranean Chicken Skewers

*These skewers are easy to assemble, and can be cooked on a grill or charcoal barbecue.*

INGREDIENTS

*Serves 4*

90ml/6 tbsp olive oil

45ml/3 tbsp fresh lemon juice

1 clove garlic, finely chopped

30ml/2 tbsp chopped fresh basil

2 medium courgettes

1 long thin aubergine

300g/11oz boneless chicken, cut into
    5cm/2in cubes

12–16 pickled onions

1 pepper, red or yellow, cut into
    5cm/2in squares

salt and black pepper

1 In a small bowl mix the oil with the lemon juice, garlic and basil. Season with salt and pepper.

2 Slice the courgettes and aubergine lengthways into strips 5mm/¹/₄in thick. Cut them crossways about two-thirds of the way along their length. Discard the shorter length. Wrap half the chicken pieces with the courgette slices, and the other half with the aubergine slices.

3 Prepare the skewers by alternating the chicken, onions and pepper pieces. Lay the prepared skewers on a platter, and sprinkle with the flavoured oil. Leave to marinate for at least 30 minutes. Preheat the grill, or prepare a barbecue.

4 Grill or barbecue for about 10 minutes, or until the vegetables are tender, turning the skewers occasionally. Serve hot.

# Chicken Paella

*There are many variations of this basic recipe. Any seasonal vegetables can be added, together with mussels and other shellfish. Serve straight from the pan.*

INGREDIENTS

*Serves 4*

4 chicken legs (thighs and drumsticks)

60ml/4 tbsp olive oil

1 large onion, finely chopped

1 garlic clove, crushed

5ml/1 tsp ground turmeric

115g/4oz chorizo sausage or smoked ham

225g/8oz/generous 1 cup long grain rice

600ml/1 pint/2$^1$/$_2$ cups chicken stock

4 tomatoes, skinned, seeded and chopped

1 red pepper, seeded and sliced

115g/4oz/1 cup frozen peas

salt and black pepper

1 Preheat the oven to 180°C/350°F/Gas 4. Cut the chicken legs in half.

2 Heat the oil in a 30cm/12in paella pan or large flameproof casserole and brown the chicken pieces on both sides. Add the onion and garlic and stir in the turmeric. Cook for 2 minutes.

3 Slice the sausage or dice the ham and add to the pan, with the rice and stock. Bring to the boil and season to taste, cover and bake for 15 minutes.

4 Remove from the oven and add the chopped tomatoes and sliced red pepper and frozen peas. Return to the oven and cook for a further 10–15 minutes or until the chicken is tender and the rice has absorbed the stock.

# Chicken Cutlets with Olives

*This quick and tasty dish makes a good light main course.*

### INGREDIENTS

*Serves 4*

90ml/6 tbsp olive oil

1 clove garlic, peeled and lightly
    crushed

1 dried chilli, lightly crushed

500g/1¼ lb boneless chicken breast,
    cut into 5mm/¼ in slices

100ml/4fl oz/½ cup dry white wine

4 tomatoes, peeled and seeded,
    cut into thin strips

about 24 black olives

6–8 leaves fresh basil, torn into pieces

salt and black pepper

1 Heat 60ml/4 tbsp of the olive oil in a large frying pan. Add the garlic and crushed dried chilli, and cook over low heat until the garlic is golden.

2 Raise the heat to moderate and add the remaining oil. Place the chicken slices in the pan, and brown them lightly on both sides for about 2 minutes. Season with salt and pepper. Remove the chicken to a heated dish.

3 Discard the garlic and chilli. Add the wine, tomato strips and olives. Cook over moderate heat for 3–4 minutes, scraping up any meat residue from the bottom of the pan.

4 Return the chicken to the pan. Sprinkle with the torn basil. Heat through for 30 seconds, and serve at once.

# Chicken in Green Sauce

*Slow, gentle cooking makes the chicken succulent and tender.*

INGREDIENTS

*Serves 4*

25g/1oz/2 tbsp butter

15ml/1 tbsp olive oil

4 chicken portions

1 small onion, finely chopped

150ml/$^1$/4 pint/$^2$/3 cup medium dry
   white wine

150ml/$^1$/4 pint/$^2$/3 cup chicken stock

175g/6oz watercress

2 thyme sprigs and 2 tarragon sprigs

150ml/$^1$/4 pint/$^2$/3 cup double cream

salt and black pepper

watercress leaves, to garnish

1 Heat the butter and oil in a heavy shallow pan, then brown the chicken evenly. Transfer the chicken to a plate using a slotted spoon and keep warm in the oven.

2 Add the onion to the cooking juices in the pan and cook until softened but not coloured.

3 Stir in the wine, boil for 2–3 minutes, then add the stock and bring to the boil. Return the chicken to the pan, cover tightly and cook very gently for about 30 minutes, until the chicken juices run clear. Then transfer the chicken to a warm dish, cover the dish and keep warm.

4 Boil the cooking juices hard until reduced to about 60ml/ 4 tbsp. Remove the leaves from the watercress and herbs, add to the pan with the cream and simmer over a medium heat until the sauce has thickened slightly.

5 Return the cooked chicken to the casserole, season and heat through for a few minutes. Garnish with watercress leaves before serving.

# Chicken and Chorizo

*The perfect way to use up leftover cold meat – this spicy dish is a fast, fortifying meal for a hungry family.*

INGREDIENTS

Serves 4

45ml/3 tbsp vegetable oil

1 medium onion, chopped

1 celery stick, chopped

$^1/_2$ red pepper, chopped

400g/14oz/2 cups long-grain rice

1 litre/1$^3/_4$ pints/4 cups chicken stock

15ml/1 tbsp tomato purée

3–4 shakes of Tabasco sauce

225g/8oz cold roast chicken or pork, thickly sliced

115g/4oz cooked sausage, such as chorizo or kabanos, sliced

75g/3oz frozen peas

1 Heat the oil in a heavy-based saucepan and add the onion, celery and pepper. Cook to soften without colouring.

2 Add the rice, chicken stock, tomato purée and Tabasco sauce. Simmer uncovered for about 10 minutes.

3 Stir in the cold meat, sausage and peas and simmer for a further 5 minutes. Switch off the heat, cover and leave to stand for 5 minutes more before serving.

### VARIATION

You could also add cooked ham, smoked cod or haddock and fresh shellfish to this dish.

# Chicken with Mushrooms

*Serve on a dish surrounded with nutty brown rice or tagliatelle verde. White wine or brandy may be used to deglaze the pan in place of sherry.*

### INGREDIENTS

*Serves 4*

4 large chicken breasts, boned and skinned

45ml/3 tbsp olive oil

1 onion, thinly sliced

1 garlic clove, crushed

225g/8oz/3 cups button mushrooms, quartered

30ml/2 tbsp sherry

15ml/1 tbsp lemon juice

150ml/¼ pint/⅔ cup single cream

salt and black pepper

3 Add the mushrooms and cook them for a further 5 minutes. Remove and keep warm.

5 Add the sherry and lemon juice to the pan and quickly return the chicken, onions, garlic and mushrooms, stirring to coat.

4 Increase the heat. Add the remaining oil and fry the chicken very quickly, in small batches for 3–4 minutes until lightly coloured. Season each batch with a little salt and freshly ground black pepper. Remove and keep warm on a plate while frying the rest of the chicken.

6 Stir in the cream and bring to the boil. Adjust the seasoning to taste. Serve immediately.

1 Divide the chicken breasts into two natural fillets. Place each between two sheets of clear film and flatten to a thickness of 5mm/¼in with a rolling pin. Cut into 2.5cm/1in diagonal strips.

2 Heat 30ml/2 tbsp of the oil in a large frying pan and cook the onion and crushed garlic slowly until tender.

# Chicken with Orange and Mustard Sauce

*The beauty of this recipe is its simplicity; the chicken continues to cook in its own juices while you prepare the sauce.*

INGREDIENTS

*Serves 4*

2 large oranges

4 chicken breasts, boned and skinned

5ml/1 tsp sunflower oil

salt and black pepper

new potatoes and sliced courgettes
  tossed in parsley, to serve

*Orange and mustard sauce*

10ml/2 tsp cornflour

150ml/$^1$/4 pint/$^2$/3 cup natural yogurt

5ml/1 tsp Dijon mustard

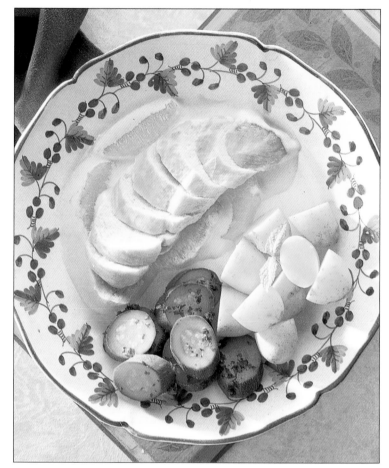

1 Peel the oranges using a sharp knife, removing all the white pith. Remove the segments by cutting between the membranes, holding the fruit over a small bowl to catch any juice. Set aside with the juice until required.

2 Season the chicken with salt and freshly ground black pepper. Heat the oil in a non-stick frying pan and cook the chicken breasts for 5 minutes on each side. Take out of the frying pan and wrap in foil; the meat will continue to cook for a while.

3 To make the sauce, blend together the cornflour with the juice from the orange. Add the yogurt and mustard. Put into the frying pan and slowly bring to the boil. Simmer for 1 minute.

4 Add the orange segments to the sauce and heat gently. Unwrap the chicken and add any excess juices to the sauce. Slice on the diagonal and serve with the sauce, new potatoes and sliced courgettes tossed in parsley.

# French-style Pot-roast Poussins

*An incredibly simple dish to make
that looks and tastes extra special.*

INGREDIENTS

*Serves 4*

15ml/1 tbsp olive oil

1 onion, sliced

1 large garlic clove, sliced

50g/2oz/scant$^1$/$_2$ cup diced lightly smoked
   bacon

2 fresh poussins (just under 450g/1lb each)

30ml/2 tbsp melted butter

2 baby celery hearts, each cut into 4

8 baby carrots

2 small courgettes, cut into chunks

8 small new potatoes

600ml/1 pint/2$^1$/$_2$ cups chicken stock

150ml/$^1$/$_4$ pint/$^2$/$_3$ cup dry white wine

1 bay leaf

2 fresh thyme sprigs

2 fresh rosemary sprigs

15g/$^1$/$_2$oz/1 tbsp butter, softened

15ml/1 tbsp plain flour

salt and black pepper

fresh herbs, to garnish

1 Preheat the oven to 190°C/
375°F/Gas 5. Heat the olive oil
in a large flameproof casserole and
add the onion, garlic and bacon.
Sauté for 5–6 minutes, until the
onions have softened.

2 Brush the poussins with a little
of the melted butter and season
well. Lay on top of the onion
mixture and arrange the prepared
vegetables around them. Add the
chicken stock, wine and herbs.

3 Cover, bake for 20 minutes,
then remove the lid and brush
the birds with the remaining
melted butter. Bake for a further
25–30 minutes until golden.

4 Transfer the poussins to a
warmed serving platter and
cut each in half with poultry shears
or scissors. Remove the vegetables
with a draining spoon and arrange
them round the birds. Cover with
foil and keep warm.

5 Discard the herbs from the pan
juices. In a bowl mix together
the butter and flour to form a
paste. Bring the liquid in the pan
to the boil and then whisk in
teaspoonfuls of the paste until
thickened. Season the sauce and
serve with the poussins and
vegetables, garnished with
fresh herbs.

# Poussins Véronique

*Double poussins are eight to ten weeks old and are large enough to serve two people.*

INGREDIENTS

*Serves 4*

2 double poussins

2 fresh tarragon or thyme sprigs

25g/1oz/2 tbsp butter

60ml/4 tbsp white wine

grated rind and juice of $^1/_2$ lemon

15ml/1 tbsp olive oil

15ml/1 tbsp plain flour

150ml/$^1/_4$ pint/$^2/_3$ cup chicken stock

115g/4oz seedless green grapes, cut in half if large

salt and black pepper

chopped fresh parsley, to garnish

1 Preheat the oven to 180°C/350°F/Gas 4. Put the herbs inside the cavity of each poussin and tie into a neat shape.

2 Heat the butter in a casserole, brown the poussins lightly all over and pour on the wine. Season, cover, and cook in the oven for 20–30 minutes or until tender.

3 Remove the poussins from the casserole and cut in half with a pair of kitchen scissors, removing the backbones and small rib cage bones. Arrange in a shallow ovenproof dish (that will slide under the grill). Sprinkle with lemon juice and brush with oil. Grill until lightly browned. Keep warm.

4 Mix the flour into the butter and wine in the casserole, and blend in the stock. Bring to the boil, season to taste and add the lemon rind and grapes, then simmer for 2–3 minutes. Spoon the sauce over the poussins, garnish with fresh parsley and serve immediately.

# Coq au Vin

*There are many variations to this traditional French dish, but this one is especially delicious. Serve it with warm French bread.*

### INGREDIENTS

*Serves 4*

30ml/2 tbsp olive oil

25g/1oz/2 tbsp butter

1.6kg/3$^1$/2lb chicken, cut into 8 pieces

115g/4oz gammon, cut into 5mm/$^1$/4in
   strips

115g/4oz button onions, peeled

115g/4oz/1$^1$/2 cups button mushrooms

2 garlic cloves, crushed

30ml/2 tbsp brandy

250ml/8fl oz/1 cup red wine

300ml/$^1$/2 pint/1$^1$/4 cups chicken stock

1 bouquet garni

25g/1oz/2 tbsp butter, blended with
   30ml/2 tbsp flour

salt and black pepper

chopped parsley, to garnish

1 Preheat the oven to 160°C/ 325°F/Gas 3. Heat the oil and butter in a large flameproof casserole and brown the chicken pieces on all sides.

2 Add the gammon strips, peeled onions, mushrooms and crushed garlic.

3 Pour over the brandy and set it alight. When the flames have subsided add the red wine, stock, bouquet garni and seasoning. Cover and cook slowly for about 1 hour in the preheated oven.

4 Remove the chicken and keep warm. Thicken the sauce with the butter mixture and season to taste. Cook for several minutes and replace the chicken. Sprinkle with chopped parsley and serve.

# Spatchcock of Poussins

*Allow one poussin per person. Serve with boiled new potatoes and salad.*

### INGREDIENTS

Serves 4

4 poussins

50g/2oz/4 tbsp butter, melted

15ml/1 tbsp lemon juice

15ml/1 tbsp chopped mixed fresh herbs,
    e.g. rosemary and parsley, plus
    extra to garnish

salt and black pepper

lemon slices, to garnish

1 Remove any trussing strings and, using a pair of kitchen scissors, cut down on either side of the backbone and remove it. Lay the poussins flat and flatten with the help of a rolling pin or mallet.

2 Thread the legs and wings on to skewers to keep the poussins flat while they are cooking.

3 Brush both sides with melted butter and season with salt and pepper to taste. Sprinkle with lemon juice and herbs.

4 Preheat the grill to medium heat and cook skin-side first for 6 minutes until golden brown. Turn over, brush with butter and grill for a further 6–8 minutes or until cooked. Garnish with more chopped herbs and lemon slices.

# Chicken in Creamy Orange Sauce

This sauce is deceptively creamy – in fact it is made with low-fat fromage frais, which is virtually fat-free. The brandy adds a richer flavour, but is optional – omit it if you prefer and use orange juice alone.

*Serves 4*

8 chicken thighs or drumsticks, skinned

45ml/3 tbsp brandy

300ml/$\frac{1}{2}$ pint/1$\frac{1}{4}$ cups orange juice

3 spring onions, chopped

10ml/2 tsp cornflour

90ml/3fl oz/$\frac{1}{3}$ cup low-fat fromage frais

salt and black pepper

rice or pasta and green salad, to serve

1 Fry the chicken pieces without fat in a non-stick or heavy pan, turning until evenly browned.

2 Stir in the brandy, orange juice and spring onions. Bring to the boil, then cover and simmer for 15 minutes, or until the chicken is tender and the juices run clear, not pink, when pierced.

3 Blend the cornflour with a little water then mix into the fromage frais. Stir this into the sauce and stir over a moderate heat until boiling.

4 Adjust the seasoning and serve with boiled rice or pasta and green salad.

---

COOK'S TIP

Cornflour helps to stabilize the fromage frais and stop it from curdling.

# Chicken Cordon Bleu

*A rich dish, popular with cheese lovers. Serve simply with green beans and tiny baked potatoes, cut and filled with cream cheese.*

INGREDIENTS

*Serves 4*

4 chicken breasts, boned and
   skinned
4 slices cooked lean ham
60ml/4 tbsp grated Gruyère or
   Emmental cheese
30ml/2 tbsp olive oil
115g/4oz button mushrooms, sliced
60ml/4 tbsp white wine
salt and black pepper
watercress, to garnish

1 Place the chicken between two pieces of clear film and flatten to a thickness of 5mm/¼in with a rolling pin. Place the chicken breasts, outer side down, on the board and lay a slice of ham on each. Divide the cheese between the chicken and season with a little salt and freshly ground pepper.

2 Fold the chicken breasts in half and secure with wooden cocktail sticks, making a large "stitch" to hold the pieces together.

3 Heat the oil in a large frying pan and brown the chicken parcels on all sides. Remove to a dish and keep warm.

4 Add the mushrooms to the pan and cook for several minutes to brown lightly. Replace the chicken and pour over the wine, cover, and cook gently for 15–20 minutes until tender. Remove the cocktail sticks and arrange on a serving dish with a bunch of watercress.

# Tuscan Chicken

This simple peasant casserole has all the flavours of traditional Tuscan ingredients. The wine can be replaced by chicken stock.

INGREDIENTS

Serves 4

8 chicken thighs, skinned

5ml/1 tsp olive oil

1 medium onion, thinly sliced

2 red peppers, seeded and sliced

1 garlic clove, crushed

300ml/¹/₂ pint/1¹/₄ cups passata

150ml/¹/₄ pint/²/₃ cup dry white wine

large sprig fresh oregano, or 5ml/1 tsp dried oregano

400g/14oz can cannellini beans, drained

45ml/3 tbsp fresh breadcrumbs

salt and black pepper

1 Fry the chicken in the oil in a non-stick or heavy pan until golden brown. Remove and keep hot. Add the onion and peppers to the pan and gently sauté until softened, but not brown. Stir in the garlic.

2 Add the chicken, passata, wine and oregano. Season well, bring to the boil then cover the pan tightly.

3 Lower the heat and simmer gently, stirring occasionally for 30–35 minutes or until the chicken is tender and the juices run clear, not pink, when pierced with the point of a knife.

4 Stir in the cannellini beans and simmer for a further 5 minutes until heated through. Sprinkle with the breadcrumbs and cook under a hot grill until golden brown.

# Crispy Spring Chickens

*These small birds can be roasted in the oven fairly quickly and are delicious either hot or cold.*

INGREDIENTS

*Serves 4*

2 x 900g/2lb chickens
salt and black pepper

*For the honey glaze*
30ml/2 tbsp clear honey
30ml/2 tbsp sherry
15ml/1 tbsp vinegar

1 Preheat the oven to 180°C/ 350°F/Gas 4. Tie the birds into a neat shape and place on a wire rack over the sink. Pour over boiling water to plump the flesh and pat dry with kitchen paper.

2 Mix the honey, sherry and vinegar together and brush over the birds. Season well.

3 Put the rack into a roasting tin and roast the birds for 45–55 minutes. Baste well during cooking with the honey glaze until crisp and golden brown.

# Spanish Chicken

*A colourful one pot dish, ideal for entertaining and delicious served with a crisp green salad.*

### INGREDIENTS

*Serves 8*

30ml/2 tbsp plain flour

10ml/2 tsp ground paprika

2.5ml/$^1$/2 tsp salt

16 chicken drumsticks

50ml/2fl oz/$^1$/4 cup olive oil

1.2 litres/2 pints/5 cups chicken stock

1 onion, finely chopped

2 garlic cloves, crushed

450g/1lb/2$^2$/3 cups long grain rice

2 bay leaves

225g/8oz/1$^1$/3 cups diced cooked ham

115g/4oz/1 cup pimento-stuffed green
   olives

1 green pepper, seeded and diced

2 x 400g/14oz cans chopped tomatoes,
   with the juice

60ml/4 tbsp chopped fresh parsley

1 Preheat the oven to 180°C/ 350°F/Gas 4. Shake together the flour, paprika and salt in a plastic bag, add the drumsticks and toss to coat.

2 Heat the oil in a large flame-proof casserole and, working in batches, brown the chicken drumsticks slowly on all sides. Remove and keep warm.

3 Meanwhile, bring the stock to the boil and add the onion, crushed garlic, rice and bay leaves. Cook for 10 minutes. Draw aside and add the ham, olives, peppers, and canned tomatoes with their juice. Transfer to a shallow ovenproof dish.

4 Arrange the chicken on top, cover and bake for 30–40 minutes or until tender. Add a little more stock if necessary to prevent from drying out. Remove the bay leaves and sprinkle over the chopped parsley to garnish.

# Lemon Chicken Stir-fry

*It is essential to prepare all the ingredients before you begin so they are ready to cook. This dish is cooked in minutes.*

## INGREDIENTS

*Serves 4*

4 chicken breasts, boned and skinned

15ml/1 tbsp light soy sauce

75ml/5 tbsp cornflour

1 bunch spring onions

1 lemon

1 garlic clove, crushed

15ml/1 tbsp caster sugar

30ml/2 tbsp sherry

150ml/¼ pint/⅔ cup chicken stock

60ml/4 tbsp olive oil

salt and black pepper

1 Divide the chicken breasts into two natural fillets. Place each between two sheets of clear film and flatten to a thickness of 5mm/¼ in with a rolling pin.

2 Cut into 2.5cm/1in strips across the grain of the fillets. Put in a bowl with the soy sauce and toss to coat. Sprinkle on 60ml/ 4 tbsp of the cornflour and toss.

3 Trim off the roots and cut the spring onions diagonally into 1cm/½in pieces. With a swivel peeler, remove the lemon rind in thin strips and cut into fine shreds, or grate finely. Reserve the lemon juice. Have ready the garlic, sugar, sherry, stock, lemon juice and remaining cornflour blended to a paste with water.

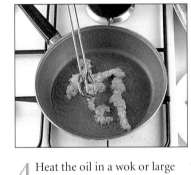

4 Heat the oil in a wok or large frying pan and cook the chicken very quickly in small batches for 3–4 minutes until lightly coloured. Remove to a dish and keep warm.

5 Add the spring onions and garlic to the pan and cook for 2 minutes.

6 Add the remaining ingredients, with chicken, and bring to the boil, stirring until thickened. Add more sherry or stock if necessary and stir until the chicken is evenly covered with sauce. Reheat for about 2 minutes.

# Chicken with Blackberries and Lemon

*This delicious stew combines some wonderful flavours. The red wine and blackberries give it a dramatic appearance.*

### INGREDIENTS

*Serves 4*

4 part-boned chicken breasts
25g/1oz/2 tbsp butter
15ml/1 tbsp sunflower oil
25g/1oz/4 tbsp flour
150ml/$^1$/4 pint/$^2$/3 cup red wine
150ml/$^1$/4 pint/$^2$/3 cup chicken stock
grated rind of $^1$/2 orange plus 15ml/1 tbsp juice
3 sprigs lemon balm, finely chopped, plus 1 sprig to garnish
150ml/$^1$/4 pint/$^2$/3 cup double cream
1 egg yolk
115g/4oz/1 cup fresh blackberries, plus 50g/2oz/$^1$/2 cup to garnish
salt and black pepper

1 Preheat the oven to 180°C/ 350°F/Gas 4. Remove any skin from the chicken, and season the meat. Heat the butter and oil in a frying pan, fry the chicken to seal it, then transfer to a casserole dish. Stir the flour into the pan, then add the wine and stock and bring to the boil. Add the orange rind and juice, and the chopped lemon balm. Pour over the chicken.

2 Cover the casserole and cook in the oven for about 40 minutes.

3 Blend the cream with the egg yolk, add some of the liquid from the casserole and stir back into the dish with the blackberries (reserving those for the garnish). Cover and cook for another 10–15 minutes. Serve garnished with the rest of the blackberries and the sprig of lemon balm.

# Chicken Pancakes

*A good way of using up leftover cooked chicken and bought pancakes.*

INGREDIENTS

*Serves 4*

225g/8oz cooked, boned chicken

25g/1oz/2 tbsp butter

1 small onion, finely chopped

50g/2oz mushrooms, finely
    chopped

30ml/2 tbsp plain flour

150ml/$^1$/4 pint/$^2$/3 cup chicken
    stock or milk

15ml/1 tbsp chopped fresh parsley

8 small or 4 large cooked pancakes

oil, for brushing

30ml/2 tbsp grated cheese

salt and black pepper

1 Remove the skin from the chicken and cut into cubes.

2 Heat the butter in a saucepan and cook the onion gently until tender. Add the mushrooms. Cook, covered, for a further 3–4 minutes.

3 Add the flour and then the stock or milk, stirring continually. Boil to thicken and simmer for 2 minutes. Season with salt and black pepper.

4 Add the chicken cubes and chopped fresh parsley.

5 Divide the filling equally between the pancakes, roll them up and arrange in a greased ovenproof dish. Preheat the grill.

6 Brush the pancakes with a little oil and sprinkle with cheese. Grill until browned. Serve hot.

# Chicken with Cajun Sauce

*Sizzling fried chicken served in a tasty tomato sauce.*

*Serves 4*

1.6kg/3$^1$/2lb chicken, cut into 8 pieces

90g/3$^1$/2oz/$^3$/4 cup plain flour

250ml/8fl oz/1 cup buttermilk or milk

vegetable oil, for frying

salt and black pepper

chopped spring onions, to garnish

*For the sauce*

115g/4oz/$^2$/3 cup lard or vegetable oil

65g/2$^1$/2oz/9 tbsp flour

2 onions, chopped

2–3 celery sticks, chopped

1 large green pepper, seeded and chopped

2 garlic cloves, finely chopped

250ml/8fl oz/1 cup passata

450ml/$^3$/4 pint/1$^7$/8 cups red wine or
  chicken stock

225g/8oz/1$^3$/4 cups tomatoes, skinned and
  chopped

2 bay leaves

15ml/1 tbsp soft brown sugar

5ml/1 tsp grated orange rind

2.5ml/$^1$/2 tsp cayenne pepper

1 To make the sauce, heat the lard or oil in a large, heavy pan and stir in the flour. Cook over moderately low heat, stirring constantly, for 15–20 minutes or until the mixture has darkened to the colour of hazelnut shells.

2 Add the chopped onions, celery, green pepper and garlic and cook, stirring, until the vegetables are softened.

3 Stir in the remaining sauce ingredients with salt and pepper to taste. Bring to the boil, then simmer for 1 hour or until the sauce is rich and thick. Stir from time to time.

4 Meanwhile, prepare the chicken. Put the flour in a plastic bag and season with salt and pepper. Dip each piece of chicken in buttermilk, then dredge in the flour to coat lightly all over. Shake off excess flour. Set the chicken aside for 20 minutes to let the coating set before frying.

5 Heat the vegetable oil 2.5cm/1in deep in a large frying pan until it is very hot and starting to sizzle. Fry the chicken pieces, turning them once, for about 30 minutes or until deep golden brown all over and cooked through.

6 Drain the chicken pieces on paper towels. Add them to the sauce and sprinkle with chopped spring onions.

# Chicken Stroganov

*Based on the classic Russian dish, usually made with fillet of beef. Serve with rice mixed with chopped celery and spring onions.*

*Serves 4*

4 large chicken breasts, boned and
   skinned
45ml/3 tbsp olive oil
1 large onion, thinly sliced
225g/8oz/3 cups mushrooms, sliced
300ml/$^1/_2$ pint/$1^1/_4$ cups soured cream
salt and black pepper
15ml/1 tbsp chopped fresh parsley,
   to garnish

1 Divide the chicken breasts into two natural fillets, place between two sheets of clear film and flatten each to a thickness of 1cm/$^1/_2$in with a rolling pin.

2 Cut into 2.5cm/1in strips diagonally across the fillets.

3 Heat 30ml/2 tbsp of the oil in a frying pan and cook the onion slowly until soft but not coloured.

4 Add the mushrooms and cook until golden brown. Remove and keep warm.

5 Increase the heat, add the remaining oil and fry the chicken very quickly, in small batches, for 3–4 minutes until lightly coloured. Remove to a dish and keep warm.

6 Return all the chicken, onions and mushrooms to the pan and season with salt and black pepper. Stir in the soured cream and bring to the boil. Sprinkle with fresh parsley and serve immediately.

# Pot-roast Chicken with Sausage Stuffing

*These casseroled chickens will be tender and succulent.*

INGREDIENTS

Serves 6

2 x 1.12kg/2¹/₂lb chickens

30ml/2 tbsp vegetable oil

350ml/12fl oz/1¹/₂ cups chicken stock or
   half wine and half stock

1 bay leaf

*For the stuffing*

450g/1lb sausagemeat

1 small onion, chopped

1–2 garlic cloves, finely chopped

5ml/1 tsp hot paprika

2.5ml/¹/₂ tsp dried chilli (optional)

2.5ml/¹/₂ tsp dried thyme

1.5ml/¹/₄ tsp ground allspice

40g/1¹/₂oz/1 cup coarse fresh breadcrumbs

1 egg, beaten to mix

salt and black pepper

1 Preheat the oven to 180°C/
350°F/Gas 4.

2 For the stuffing, put the
sausagemeat, onion and garlic
in a frying pan and fry over
moderate heat until the sausagemeat is lightly browned and
crumbly, stirring and turning so it
cooks evenly. Remove from the
heat and mix in the remaining
stuffing ingredients with salt and
pepper to taste.

3 Divide the stuffing between the
chickens, packing it into the
body cavities (or, if preferred, stuff
the neck end and bake the leftover
stuffing in a separate dish). Truss
the birds.

4 Heat the oil in a flameproof
casserole just big enough to
hold the chickens. Brown the birds
all over.

5 Add the stock and bay leaf and
season. Cover and bring to the
boil, then transfer to the oven. Pot-
roast for 1¹/₄ hours or until the
birds are cooked (the juices will
run clear).

6 Untruss the chickens and
spoon the stuffing on to a
serving platter. Arrange the birds
and serve with the strained
cooking liquid.

### VARIATION

For Pot-roast Guinea Fowl, use 2
guinea fowl instead of chickens.

# Chicken with Asparagus

*Canned asparagus may be used instead of fresh, but will not require any cooking – simply add at the very end to warm through.*

INGREDIENTS

*Serves 4*

4 large chicken breasts, boned and
   skinned
15ml/1 tbsp ground coriander
30ml/2 tbsp olive oil
20 slender asparagus spears, cut
   into 7.5–10cm/3–4 in lengths
300ml/$\frac{1}{2}$ pint/1$\frac{1}{4}$ cups chicken stock
15ml/1 tbsp cornflour
15ml/1 tbsp lemon juice
salt and black pepper
15ml/1 tbsp chopped fresh parsley

1 Divide the chicken breasts into two natural fillets. Place each between two sheets of clear film and flatten to a thickness of 5mm/$\frac{1}{4}$ in with a rolling pin. Cut into 2.5cm/1in strips diagonally. Sprinkle over the coriander and toss to coat each piece.

2 Heat the oil in a large frying pan and fry the chicken very quickly in small batches for 3–4 minutes until lightly coloured. Season each batch with a little salt and freshly ground black pepper. Remove and keep warm while frying the rest of the chicken.

3 Add the asparagus and chicken stock to the pan and bring to the boil. Cook for a further 4–5 minutes, or until tender.

4 Mix the cornflour to a paste with a little cold water and stir into the sauce to thicken. Return the chicken to the pan and add the lemon juice. Reheat and then serve immediately, garnished with fresh parsley.

# Poussins Waldorf

*Sunday roast and stuffing, with a
difference.*

INGREDIENTS

*Serves 6*

6 poussins, each weighing about
    500g/1$^1$/4lb
salt and black pepper
40–50g/1$^1$/2–2oz/3–4 tbsp butter, melted

*For the stuffing*
25g/1oz/2 tbsp butter
1 onion, finely chopped
300g/11oz/2$^1$/4 cups cooked rice
2 celery sticks, finely chopped
2 red apples, cored and finely diced
50g/2oz/$^1$/3 cup walnuts, chopped
75ml/5 tbsp cream sherry or apple juice
30ml/2 tbsp lemon juice

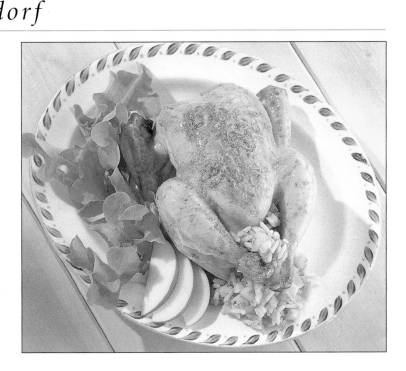

1 Preheat the oven to 180°C/
350°F/Gas 4. To make the
stuffing, melt the butter in a small
frying pan and fry the onion,
stirring occasionally, until soft. Tip
the onion and butter into a bowl
and add the remaining stuffing
ingredients. Season with salt and
pepper and mix well.

2 Divide the stuffing among the
poussins, stuffing the body
cavities. Truss the birds and
arrange in a roasting tin. Sprinkle
with salt and pepper and drizzle
over the melted butter.

3 Roast for about 1$^1$/4–1$^1$/2 hours.
Untruss before serving.

## CARVING POULTRY

Carving a bird neatly for serving makes the presenta-
tion attractive. You will need a sharp long-bladed
knife, or an electric knife, plus a long 2-pronged fork
and a carving board with a well to catch the juices.

Cut away any trussing string. For a stuffed bird,
spoon the stuffing from the cavity into a serving
dish. For easier carving, remove the wishbone.

Insert the fork into one breast to hold the bird
steady. Cut through the skin to the ball and socket
joint on that side of the body, then slice through it to
sever the leg from the body. Repeat on the other side.

1 Slice through the ball and socket joint in each leg
to sever the thigh and drumstick. If carving
turkey, slice the meat off the thigh and drumstick,
parallel to the bone, turning to get even slices; leave
chicken thighs and drumsticks whole.

2 To carve the breast of a turkey or chicken, cut
5mm/$^1$/4in thick slices at an angle, slicing down
on both sides of the breastbone. For smaller birds,
remove the meat on each side of the breastbone in a
single piece, then slice across.

# Oat-crusted Chicken with Sage

*Oats make a good coating for savoury foods, and offer a good way to add extra fibre.*

*Serves 4*

45ml/3 tbsp skimmed milk

10ml/2 tsp English mustard

40g/1¹/₂oz/¹/₂ cup rolled oats

45ml/3 tbsp chopped sage leaves

8 chicken thighs or drumsticks, skinned

115g/4oz/¹/₂ cup low-fat fromage frais

5ml/1 tsp wholegrain mustard

salt and black pepper

fresh sage leaves, to garnish

---

### COOK'S TIP

If fresh sage is not available, choose another fresh herb, such as thyme or parsley, rather than a dried alternative.

---

1 Preheat the oven to 200°C/ 400°F/Gas 6. Mix together the milk and English mustard.

2 Mix the oats with 30ml/2 tbsp of the sage and the seasoning on a plate. Brush the chicken with the milk and press into the oats.

3 Place the chicken on a baking sheet and bake for about 40 minutes, or until the juices run clear, not pink, when pierced through the thickest part.

4 Meanwhile, mix together the low-fat fromage frais, whole-grain mustard, remaining sage and seasoning, then serve with the chicken. Garnish the chicken with fresh sage and serve hot or cold.

# Chicken with Sage, Prunes and Brandy

*This stir-fry has a very rich sauce based on a good brandy – use the best you can afford.*

### INGREDIENTS

*Serves 4*

115g/4oz prunes

1.5kg/3–3¹/₂lb boneless chicken breast

300ml/¹/₂ pint/1¹/₄ cups cognac or brandy

15ml/1 tbsp fresh sage, chopped

150g/5oz smoked bacon, in one piece

50g/2oz/4 tbsp butter

24 baby onions, peeled and quartered

salt and black pepper

fresh sage sprigs, to garnish

1 Stone the prunes and cut them into slivers. Remove the skin from the chicken and cut the breast into thin pieces.

2 Mix together the prunes, chicken, cognac and chopped sage in a non-metallic dish. Cover and leave to marinate overnight.

3 Next day, strain the chicken and prunes, reserving the cognac marinade mixture, and pat dry on kitchen towels.

4 Cut the smoked bacon into dice and set aside.

5 Heat the wok and add half the butter. When melted, add the onions and stir-fry for 4 minutes until crisp and golden. Set aside.

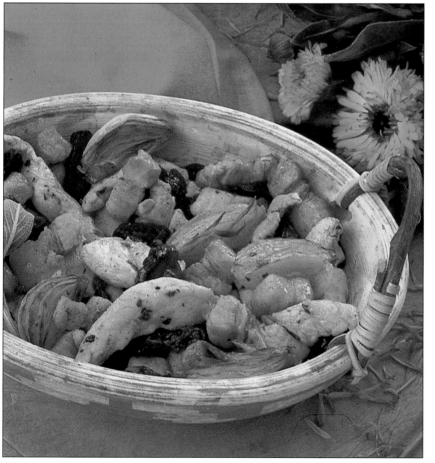

6 Add the bacon to the wok and stir-fry for 1 minute until it begins to release some fat. Add the remaining butter and stir-fry the chicken and prunes for 3–4 minutes until crisp and golden. Push the chicken mixture to one side in the wok, add the cognac and simmer until thickened. Stir the chicken into the sauce, season well with salt and pepper, and serve garnished with sage.

# Minty Yogurt Chicken

*Chicken marinated with yogurt, mint, lemon and honey and grilled.*

## INGREDIENTS

*Serves 4*

8 chicken thigh portions, skinned
15ml/1 tbsp clear honey
30ml/2 tbsp lime or lemon juice
30ml/2 tbsp natural yogurt
60ml/4 tbsp chopped fresh mint
salt and black pepper
new potatoes and a tomato salad,
   to serve

1 Slash the chicken flesh at regular intervals with a sharp knife. Place in a bowl.

2 Mix together the honey, lime or lemon juice, yogurt, seasoning and half the mint.

3 Spoon the marinade over the chicken and leave to marinate for 30 minutes. Line the grill pan with foil and cook the chicken under a moderately hot grill until thoroughly cooked and golden brown, turning the chicken occasionally during cooking.

4 Sprinkle with the remaining mint and serve with the potatoes and tomato salad.

# Chicken with Sloe Gin and Juniper

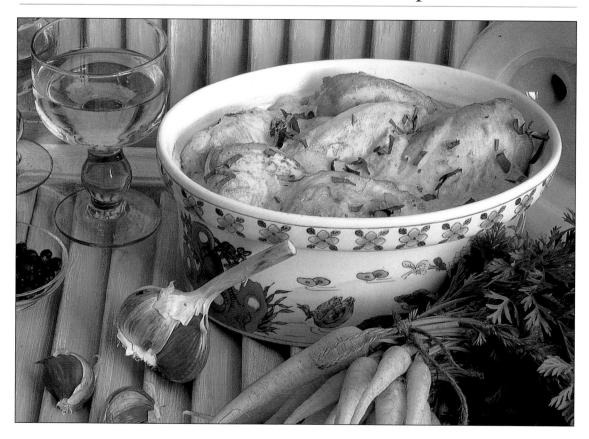

*Juniper is used in the manufacture of gin, and the reinforcement of the flavour by using both sloe gin and juniper is delicious. Sloe gin is easy to make, but can also be bought ready-made.*

## INGREDIENTS

*Serves 8*

25g/1oz/2 tbsp butter

30ml/2 tbsp sunflower oil

8 chicken breast fillets

350g/12oz carrots, cooked

1 clove garlic, crushed

15ml/1 tbsp finely chopped parsley

50ml/2fl oz/$^1$/4 cup chicken stock

50ml/2fl oz/$^1$/4 cup red wine

50ml/2fl oz/$^1$/4 cup sloe gin

5ml/1 tsp crushed juniper berries

salt and black pepper

chopped fresh basil, to garnish

1 Melt the butter with the oil in a frying pan, and fry the chicken until browned on all sides.

2 In a food processor or blender, combine all the remaining ingredients except the basil, and blend to a smooth purée. If the mixture seems too thick add a little more red wine or water.

3 Put the chicken breast in a clean pan, pour the sauce over the top and cook over a medium heat until the chicken is cooked through – about 15 minutes. Adjust the seasoning and serve garnished with chopped fresh basil.

# Chicken with Herbs and Lentils

*Chicken baked on lentils and served topped with garlic butter.*

INGREDIENTS

*Serves 4*

115g/4oz piece of thick bacon or belly
    pork, rind removed, chopped

1 large onion, sliced

475ml/16fl oz/2 cups well-flavoured
    chicken stock

bay leaf

2 sprigs each parsley, marjoram and
    thyme

225g/8oz/1 cup green or brown lentils

4 chicken portions

salt and black pepper

25–50g/1–2oz/2–4 tbsp garlic butter

### COOK'S TIP

For economy buy a smallish
chicken and cut it in quarters, to
give generous portions.

1 Fry the bacon gently in a large, heavy-based flameproof casserole until all the fat runs out and the bacon begins to brown. Add the onion and fry for about another 2 minutes.

2 Stir in the chicken stock, bay leaf, herb stalks and some of the leafy parts (keep some herb sprigs for garnish), lentils and seasoning. Preheat the oven to 190°C/375°F/ Gas 5.

3 Fry the chicken portions in a frying pan to brown the skin before placing on top of the lentils. Sprinkle with seasoning and some of the herbs.

4 Cover the casserole and cook in the oven for about 40 minutes. Serve with a knob of garlic butter on each portion and a few of the remaining herb sprigs.

# Chicken with Figs and Mint

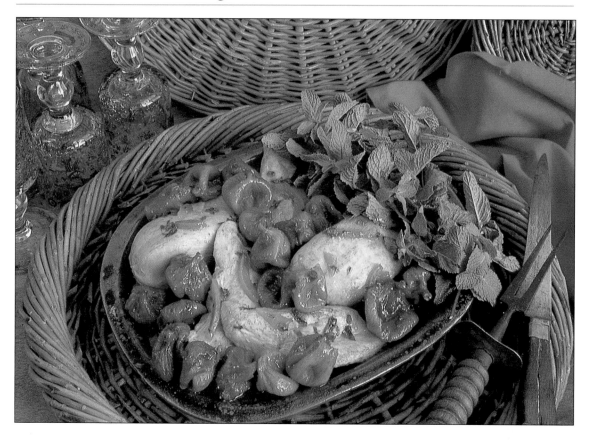

*Refreshing mint and orange flavours go well with chicken.*

INGREDIENTS

*Serves 4*

500g/1¹/₄lb/3¹/₃ cups dried figs

¹/₂ bottle sweet, fruity white wine

4 boneless chicken breasts, about
   175–225g/6–8oz each

15ml/1 tbsp butter

30ml/2 tbsp dark orange marmalade

10 mint leaves, finely chopped, plus a few
   more to garnish

juice of ¹/₂ lemon

salt and black pepper

1 Place the figs in a pan with the wine and bring to the boil, then simmer very gently for about 1 hour. Leave to cool and refrigerate overnight.

2 Fry the chicken breasts in the butter until they are cooked. Remove and keep warm. Drain any fat from the pan and pour in the juice from the figs. Boil and reduce to about 150ml/¹/₄ pint/²/₃ cup.

3 Add the marmalade, chopped mint leaves and lemon juice, and simmer for a few minutes. Season to taste. When the sauce is thick and shiny, pour it over the meat, garnish with the figs and mint leaves and serve.

# Thai Chicken and Vegetable Stir-fry

*Make this speedy dish a little hotter by adding more fresh root ginger.*

### INGREDIENTS

*Serves 4*

1 piece lemon grass (or the rind of
$^1/_2$ lemon), cut in thin slices

1cm/$^1/_2$ in piece of fresh
root ginger

1 large garlic clove

30ml/2 tbsp sunflower oil

275g/10oz lean chicken, thinly sliced

$^1/_2$ red pepper, seeded and sliced

$^1/_2$ green pepper, seeded and sliced

4 spring onions, chopped

2 medium carrots, cut into matchsticks

115g/4oz fine green beans

30ml/2 tbsp oyster sauce

pinch sugar

salt and black pepper

25g/1oz/$^1/_4$ cup salted peanuts,
lightly crushed, and coriander
leaves, to garnish

cooked rice, to serve

1 Thinly slice the lemon grass or lemon rind. Peel and chop the ginger and garlic. Heat the oil in a frying pan over a high heat. Add the lemon grass or lemon rind, ginger and garlic, and stir-fry for 30 seconds until brown.

2 Add the chicken and stir-fry for 2 minutes. Then add the vegetables and stir-fry for 4–5 minutes, until the chicken is cooked and the vegetables are almost cooked.

3 Finally stir in the oyster sauce, sugar and seasoning to taste and stir-fry for another minute to mix and blend well. Serve at once, sprinkled with the peanuts and coriander leaves and accompanied with cooked rice.

# Penne with Chicken and Ham Sauce

*A meal in itself, this colourful pasta sauce is perfect for lunch or dinner.*

## INGREDIENTS

*Serves 4*

350g/12oz/3 cups penne pasta

25g/1oz/2 tbsp butter

1 onion, chopped

1 garlic clove, chopped

1 bay leaf

475ml/16 fl oz/2 cups dry white wine

150ml/$^1$/4 pint/$^2$/3 cup crème fraîche

225g/8oz/1$^1$/2 cups cooked chicken, skinned, boned and diced

115g/4oz/$^2$/3 cup cooked lean ham, diced

115g/4oz/1 cup Gouda cheese, grated

15ml/1 tbsp chopped fresh mint

salt and black pepper

finely shredded fresh mint, to garnish

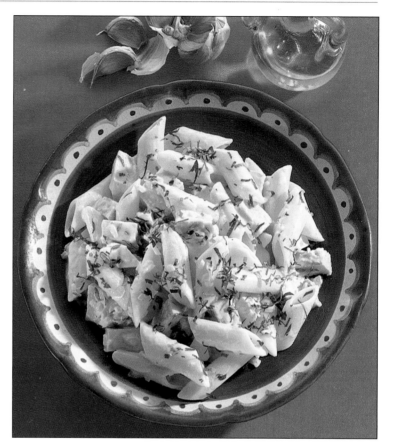

1 Cook the pasta in plenty of water following the instructions on the packet.

2 Heat the butter in a large frying pan and fry the onion for 10 minutes until softened.

### COOK'S TIP

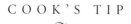

Crème fraîche is a richer, full-fat French cream with a slightly acidic taste. If you can't find any, substitute soured cream.

3 Add the garlic, bay leaf and wine and bring to the boil. Boil rapidly until reduced by half. Remove the bay leaf, then stir in the crème fraîche and bring back to the boil.

4 Add the chicken, ham and cheese and simmer for 5 minutes, stirring occasionally until heated through.

5 Add the mint and seasoning. Drain the pasta and turn it into a large serving bowl. Toss with the sauce immediately and garnish with shredded mint.

# Crunchy Stuffed Chicken Breasts

*These can be prepared ahead of time as long as the stuffing is quite cold before the chicken is stuffed. It is an ideal dish for entertaining.*

INGREDIENTS

*Serves 4*

4 chicken breasts, boned

25g/1oz/2 tbsp butter

1 garlic clove, crushed

15ml/1 tbsp Dijon mustard

*For the stuffing*

15g/$^{1}/_{2}$ oz/1 tbsp butter

1 bunch spring onions, sliced

45ml/3 tbsp fresh breadcrumbs

25g/1oz/2 tbsp pine nuts

1 egg yolk

15ml/1 tbsp chopped fresh parsley

salt and black pepper

60ml/4 tbsp grated cheese

*For the topping*

2 bacon rashers, finely chopped

50g/2oz/1 cup fresh breadcrumbs

15ml/1 tbsp grated Parmesan cheese

15ml/1 tbsp chopped fresh parsley

1 Preheat the oven to 200°C/ 400°F/Gas 6. To make the stuffing, heat 15g/$^{1}/_{2}$ oz/1 tbsp of the butter in a frying pan and cook the spring onions until soft. Remove from the heat and allow to cool for a few minutes.

2 Add the remaining ingredients and mix thoroughly.

3 To make the topping, fry the chopped bacon until crispy, drain and add to the breadcrumbs, Parmesan cheese and fresh parsley.

4 Carefully cut a deep pocket in each of the chicken breasts, using a sharp knife.

5 Divide the stuffing into four and use to fill the pockets. Put in a buttered ovenproof dish.

6 Melt the remaining butter, mix it with the crushed garlic and mustard, and brush liberally over the chicken. Press on the topping and bake uncovered for about 30–40 minutes, or until tender.

# Tagliatelle with Chicken and Herb Sauce

*This wine-flavoured sauce is best served with green salad.*

### INGREDIENTS

*Serves 4*

30ml/2 tbsp olive oil

1 red onion, cut into wedges

350g/12oz tagliatelle

1 garlic clove, chopped

350g/12oz/2$^{1}/_{2}$ cups chicken, diced

300ml/$^{1}/_{2}$ pint/1$^{1}/_{4}$ cups dry vermouth

45ml/3 tbsp chopped fresh mixed herbs

150ml/$^{1}/_{4}$ pint/$^{2}/_{3}$ cup fromage frais

salt and black pepper

shredded fresh mint, to garnish

1 Heat the oil in a large frying pan and fry the onion for 10 minutes until softened and the layers separate.

2 Cook the pasta in plenty of water following the instructions on the packet.

### COOK'S TIP

If you don't want to use vermouth, use dry white wine instead. Orvieto and frascati are two Italian wines that are ideal to use in this sauce.

3 Add the garlic and chicken to the pan and fry for 10 minutes, stirring occasionally until the chicken is browned all over and cooked through.

4 Pour in the vermouth, bring to the boil and boil rapidly until reduced by about half.

5 Stir in the herbs, fromage frais and seasoning and heat through gently, but do not boil.

6 Drain the pasta thoroughly and toss it with the sauce to coat. Serve immediately, garnished with shredded fresh mint.

# Chicken Lasagne

*Based on the Italian beef lasagne, this is an excellent dish for entertaining guests of all ages. Serve simply with a green salad.*

INGREDIENTS

*Serves 8*

30ml/2 tbsp olive oil

900g/2lb minced raw chicken

225g/8oz/1$^1$/2 cups rindless streaky bacon
   rashers, chopped

2 garlic cloves, crushed

450g/1lb leeks, sliced

225g/8oz/1$^1$/4 cups carrots, diced

30ml/2 tbsps tomato purée

475ml/16fl oz/2 cups chicken stock

12 sheets (no need to pre-cook)
   lasagne verde

*For the cheese sauce*

50g/2oz/4 tbsp butter

50g/2oz/$^1$/2 cup plain flour

600ml/1 pint/2$^1$/2 cups milk

115g/4oz/1 cup grated mature
   Cheddar cheese

1.5ml/$^1$/4 tsp dry English mustard

salt and black pepper

1 Heat the oil in a large flame-proof casserole dish and brown the minced chicken and bacon briskly, separating the pieces with a wooden spoon. Add the crushed garlic cloves, sliced leeks and diced carrots and cook for about 5 minutes until softened. Add the tomato purée, stock and seasoning. Bring to the boil, cover and simmer for 30 minutes.

2 To make the sauce, melt the butter in a saucepan, add the flour and gradually blend in the milk, stirring until smooth. Bring to the boil, stirring all the time until thickened and simmer for several minutes. Add half the grated cheese and the mustard and season to taste.

3 Preheat the oven to 190°C/375°F/Gas 5. Layer the chicken mixture, lasagne and half the cheese sauce in a 2.5 litre/5 pint ovenproof dish, starting and finishing with a layer of chicken.

4 Pour the remaining half of the cheese sauce over the top to cover, sprinkle over the remaining cheese and bake in the preheated oven for 1 hour, or until bubbling and lightly browned on top.

# SALADS
# & BARBECUES

# Monday Savoury Omelette

*Use up all the leftover odds and ends in this tasty omelette.*

INGREDIENTS

*Serves 4–6*

30ml/2 tbsp olive oil

1 large onion, chopped

2 large garlic cloves, crushed

115g/4oz rindless bacon, chopped

50g/2oz cold cooked chicken, chopped

115g/4oz leftover cooked vegetables
   (preferably ones which are not too soft)

115g/4oz/1 cup leftover cooked
   rice or pasta

4 eggs

30ml/2 tbsp chopped, mixed fresh herbs,
   such as parsley, chives, marjoram or
   tarragon, or 10ml/2 tsp dried

5ml/1 tsp Worcestershire sauce,
   or more to taste

15ml/1 tbsp grated mature
   Cheddar cheese

salt and black pepper

1 Heat the oil in a large flame-proof frying pan and sauté the onion, garlic and bacon until all the fat has run out of the bacon.

2 Add the chopped meat, vegetables and rice. Beat the eggs, herbs and Worcestershire sauce together with seasoning. Pour over the rice or pasta and vegetables, stir lightly, then leave the mixture undisturbed to cook gently for about 5 minutes.

3 When just beginning to set, sprinkle with the cheese and place under a preheated grill until just firm and golden.

### COOK'S TIP

This is surprisingly good cold, so is perfect for taking on picnics, or using for packed lunches.

# Indonesian-style Satay Chicken

*Use boneless chicken thighs to give a good flavour to these satays.*

INGREDIENTS

*Serves 4*

50g/2oz/$^1$/2 cup raw peanuts

45ml/3 tbsp vegetable oil

small onion, finely chopped

2.5cm/1in piece fresh root ginger, peeled and finely chopped

1 clove garlic, crushed

675g/1$^1$/2lb chicken thighs, skinned and cut into cubes

130g/3$^1$/2oz creamed coconut, roughly chopped

15ml/1 tbsp chilli sauce

60ml/2fl oz/$^1$/4 cup crunchy peanut butter

5ml/1 tsp soft dark brown sugar

150ml/$^1$/4 pint/$^2$/3 cup milk

1.5ml/$^1$/4 tsp salt

1 Shell and rub the skins from the peanuts, then soak them in a bowl with enough water to cover them, for 1 minute. Drain the peanuts and carefully cut them into fine slivers.

2 Heat a wok or large frying pan and add 5ml/1 tsp of the oil. When the oil is hot, stir-fry the peanuts for 1 minute until crisp and golden. Remove them with a slotted spoon and drain on kitchen paper.

3 Add the remaining oil to the hot wok. When the oil is hot, add the onion, ginger and garlic and stir-fry for 2–3 minutes until softened but not browned. Remove and drain on kitchen paper.

4 Add the chicken and stir-fry for 3–4 minutes until crisp on all sides.

5 Thread on to pre-soaked bamboo skewers and keep warm in a low oven.

6 Add the creamed coconut to the hot wok in small pieces and stir-fry until melted. Add the chilli sauce, peanut butter and cooked onion, ginger and garlic, and simmer for 2 minutes. Stir in the sugar, milk and salt and simmer for a further 3 minutes. Serve the skewered chicken hot, with a dash of the hot dipping sauce sprinkled with the peanuts.

# Chicken Spirals

*These little spirals look impressive, but they're very simple to make, and a good way to pep up plain chicken.*

INGREDIENTS

INGREDIENTS

*Serves 4*

4 chicken breasts, about
   90g/3$^1$/$_2$ oz each

20ml/4 tsp tomato purée

15g/$^1$/$_2$ oz/$^1$/$_2$ cup large basil
   leaves

1 garlic clove, crushed

15ml/1 tbsp skimmed milk

30ml/2 tbsp wholemeal flour

salt and black pepper

passata or fresh tomato sauce and
   pasta, to serve

1 Place the chicken breasts on a board. If too thick, flatten them slightly by beating with a rolling pin or meat mallet.

2 Spread each chicken breast with tomato purée, then top with a few basil leaves, a little crushed garlic and seasoning.

3 Roll up firmly around the filling and secure with a cocktail stick. Brush with milk and sprinkle with flour to coat lightly.

4 Place the spirals on a foil-lined grill pan. Cook under a medium-hot grill for 15–20 minutes, turning them occasionally, until thoroughly cooked. Serve hot, sliced, with a spoonful or two of passata or fresh tomato sauce and accompanied with pasta sprinkled with fresh basil.

### COOK'S TIP

When flattening the chicken breasts with a rolling pin, place them between two sheets of clear film.

# Chicken Pittas with Red Coleslaw

*Pittas are convenient for simple snacks and packed lunches and it's easy to pack them with lots of fresh, healthy ingredients.*

## INGREDIENTS

*Serves 4*

1/4 red cabbage

1 small red onion, finely sliced

2 radishes, thinly sliced

1 red apple, peeled, cored and grated

15ml/1 tbsp lemon juice

45ml/3 tbsp fromage frais

1 cooked chicken breast without skin, about 175g/6oz

4 large pittas or 8 small pittas

salt and black pepper

chopped fresh parsley, to garnish

1 Remove the tough central spine from the cabbage leaves, then finely shred the leaves using a large sharp knife. Place the shredded cabbage in a bowl and stir in the onion, radishes, apple and lemon juice.

2 Stir the fromage frais into the shredded cabbage mixture and season well with salt and pepper. Thinly slice the cooked chicken breast and stir into the shredded cabbage mixture until well coated in fromage frais.

3 Sprinkle the pittas with a little water, then warm them under a hot grill, then split them along one edge using a round-bladed knife. Share the filling equally among the pittas, then garnish with chopped fresh parsley.

### COOK'S TIP

If the filled pittas need to be made more than an hour in advance, line the pitta breads with crisp lettuce leaves before adding the filling.

# Chicken with Yellow Pepper Sauce

*Escalopes of chicken filled with garlic cheese with yellow pepper sauce.*

INGREDIENTS

*Serves 4*

30ml/2 tbsp olive oil

2 large yellow peppers, seeded and
    chopped

1 small onion, chopped

15ml/1 tbsp freshly squeezed orange juice

300ml/$^1$/2 pint/1$^1$/4 cups chicken stock

4 chicken breasts

75g/3oz Boursin or garlic cream cheese

12 fresh basil leaves

25g/1oz/2 tbsp butter

salt and black pepper

1 To make the yellow pepper sauce, heat half the oil in a pan and gently fry the peppers and onion until beginning to soften. Add the orange juice and stock and cook until very soft.

2 Meanwhile, lay the chicken fillets out flat and beat them out lightly.

3 Spread the chicken fillets with the Boursin or garlic cream cheese. Chop half the basil and sprinkle on top, then roll up the fillets, tucking in the ends like an envelope, and secure neatly with half a cocktail stick.

4 Heat the remaining oil and the butter in a frying pan and fry the fillets for 7–8 minutes, turning them frequently, until golden and cooked through.

5 While the fillets are cooking, press the pepper mixture through a sieve, or blend until smooth, then strain back into the pan. Season to taste and warm through, or serve cold, with the fillets, garnished with the remaining basil leaves.

---

COOK'S TIP

Turkey or veal escalopes could be
used in place of the chicken,
if you prefer.

---

# Dijon Chicken Salad

*An attractive dish to serve for lunch with herb and garlic bread.*

INGREDIENTS

Serves 4

4 chicken breasts, boned and skinned
mixed salad leaves, e.g. frisée and oakleaf
 lettuce or radicchio, to serve

*For the marinade*
30ml/2 tbsp Dijon mustard
3 garlic cloves, crushed
15ml/1 tbsp grated onion
60ml/4 tbsp white wine

*For the mustard dressing*
30ml/2 tbsp tarragon wine vinegar
5ml/1 tsp Dijon mustard
5ml/1 tsp clear honey
90ml/6 tbsp olive oil
salt and black pepper

1 Mix all the marinade ingredients together in a shallow glass or earthenware dish that is large enough to hold the chicken in a single layer.

2 Turn the chicken over in the marinade to coat completely, cover with clear film and then chill in the fridge overnight.

3 Preheat the oven to 190°C/375°F/Gas 5. Transfer the chicken and the marinade into an ovenproof dish, cover with foil and bake for about 35 minutes or until tender. Leave to cool.

4 Put all the mustard dressing ingredients into a screw-topped jar, shake vigorously to emulsify, and adjust the seasoning. (This can be made several days in advance and stored in the fridge.)

5 Slice the chicken thinly, fan out the slices and arrange on a serving dish with the salad leaves.

6 Spoon over some of the mustard dressing and serve.

# Chicken Roule

A relatively simple dish to prepare, this recipe uses mince as a filling. It is rolled in chicken meat which is spread with a creamy garlic cheese that just melts in the mouth.

## INGREDIENTS

*Serves 4*

4 boneless chicken breasts, about
    115g/4oz each
115g/4oz/1 cup minced beef
30ml/2 tbsp chopped fresh chives
225g/8oz Boursin or garlic
    cream cheese
30ml/2 tbsp clear honey
salt and black pepper

1 Preheat the oven to 190°C/ 375°F/Gas 5. Place the chicken breasts, side by side, between two pieces of clear film. Beat with a meat mallet until 1cm/¹/₂in thick and joined together.

2 Place the minced beef in a large pan. Fry for 3 minutes, add the fresh chives and seasoning. Cool.

3 Place the chicken on a board and spread with the cream cheese.

4 Top with the mince mixture, spreading it over evenly.

5 Roll up the chicken tightly to form a sausage shape.

6 Brush with honey and place in a roasting tin. Cook for 1 hour in the preheated oven. Remove from the tin and slice thinly. Serve with freshly cooked vegetables.

# Chicken Liver Kebabs

*These may be barbecued outdoors
and served with salads and baked
potatoes or grilled indoors and
served with rice and broccoli.*

INGREDIENTS

*Serves 4*

115g/4oz rindless streaky bacon rashers

350g/12oz chicken livers

12 large ready-to-eat stoned prunes

12 cherry tomatoes

8 button mushrooms

30ml/2 tbsp olive oil

1 Cut each rasher of bacon into two pieces, wrap a piece around each chicken liver and secure in position with wooden cocktail sticks.

2 Wrap the stoned prunes around the cherry tomatoes.

3 Thread the bacon-wrapped livers on to metal skewers with the tomatoes, prunes and mushrooms. Brush with oil. Cover the tomatoes and prunes with a strip of foil to protect them while grilling or barbecuing. Cook for 5 minutes on each side.

4 Remove the cocktail sticks and serve the kebabs immediately.

# Pancake Parcels

*Making good use of the different types of minced poultry now available, these quick and easy pancakes are filled with a delicious chicken and apple mixture.*

INGREDIENTS

*Serves 4*

*For the filling*

30ml/2 tbsp oil

450g/1lb/4 cups minced chicken

30ml/2 tbsp chopped fresh chives

2 green eating apples, cored and
  diced

25g/1oz/4 tbsp flour

175ml/6fl oz/³/4 cup chicken stock

salt and black pepper

*For the pancakes*

115g/4oz/1 cup plain flour

pinch of salt

1 egg, beaten

300ml/¹/2 pint/1¹/4 cups milk

oil for frying

*For the sauce*

60ml/4 tbsp cranberry sauce

50ml/2fl oz/¹/4 cup chicken stock

15ml/1 tbsp clear honey

15g/¹/2 oz/2 tbsp cornflour

1 To make the filling, heat the oil in a large pan and fry the chicken for 5 minutes. Add the chives and apples and then the flour. Stir in the stock and seasoning. Cook for 20 minutes.

2 To make the pancakes, sift the flour into a bowl together with a pinch of salt. Make a well in the centre and drop in the egg. Beat it in gradually with the milk to form a smooth batter. Heat the oil in a 15cm/6in omelette pan. Pour off the oil and add one-quarter of the pancake mixture. Tilt the pan to cover the base with the mixture and cook for 2–3 minutes. Turn the pancake over and cook for a further 2 minutes. Stack each pancake on top of one another and keep warm.

3 For the sauce, put the cranberry sauce, stock and honey into a pan. Heat gently until melted. Blend the cornflour with 20ml/4 tsp cold water, stir it in and bring to the boil. Cook, stirring until clear.

4 Lay the pancakes on a chopping board, spoon the filling into the centre and fold over around the filling. Put on a plate and spoon on the sauce. Serve with a fresh green vegetable.

# Citrus Kebabs

*Serve on a bed of lettuce leaves and garnish with fresh mint and orange and lemon slices.*

INGREDIENTS

*Serves 4*

4 chicken breasts, skinned and boned
sprigs of fresh mint, to garnish
orange, lemon or lime slices, to garnish
   (optional)

*For the marinade*
finely grated rind and juice of $^1/_2$ orange
finely grated rind and juice of $^1/_2$ small
   lemon or lime
30ml/2 tbsp olive oil
30ml/2 tbsp clear honey
30ml/2 tbsp chopped fresh mint
1.5ml/$^1/_4$ tsp ground cumin
salt and black pepper

1 Cut the chicken into cubes of approximately 2.5cm/1in.

2 Mix the marinade ingredients together in a glass or ceramic bowl, add the chicken cubes and leave to marinate for at least 2 hours.

3 Thread the chicken pieces on to skewers and grill or barbecue over low coals for 15 minutes, basting with the marinade and turning frequently. Serve garnished with extra mint and citrus slices if desired.

# MIDWEEK
# MEALS

# Chicken Satay

*Marinate in the satay sauce overnight to allow the flavours to penetrate the chicken. Soak wooden skewers in water overnight to prevent them from burning while cooking.*

## INGREDIENTS

*Serves 4*

4 chicken breasts

lemon slices, to garnish

lettuce leaves, to serve

spring onions, to serve

*For the satay*

115g/4oz/$^1/_2$ cup crunchy peanut butter

1 small onion, chopped

1 garlic clove, crushed

30ml/2 tbsp chutney

60ml/4 tbsp olive oil

5ml/1 tsp light soy sauce

30ml/2 tbsp lemon juice

1.5ml/$^1/_4$ tsp chilli powder or cayenne
   pepper

1 Put all the satay ingredients into a food processor or blender and process until smooth. Spoon into a large dish.

2 Remove all bone and skin from the chicken and cut into 2.5cm/1in cubes. Add to the satay mixture and stir to coat the chicken pieces. Cover with clear film and chill for at least 4 hours or, better still, overnight.

3 Preheat the grill or barbecue. Thread the chicken pieces on to the satay sticks.

4 Cook for 10 minutes, brushing occasionally with the satay sauce. Serve on a bed of lettuce with spring onions and garnish with lemon slices.

# Spicy Chicken Canapés

*These tiny little cocktail sandwiches have a spicy filling, and are finished with different toppings. Use square bread so that you can cut out more rounds and have less wastage.*

INGREDIENTS

*Makes 18*

75g/3oz/³/4 cup finely chopped
   cooked chicken

2 spring onions, finely chopped

30ml/2 tbsp chopped red pepper

90ml/6 tbsp Curry Mayonnaise

6 slices white bread

15ml/1 tbsp paprika

15ml/1 tbsp chopped fresh parsley

30ml/2 tbsp chopped salted
   peanuts

2 Spread the mixture over three of the bread slices and sandwich with the remaining bread, pressing well together. Spread the remaining Curry Mayonnaise over the top and cut into 4cm/1¹/2in circles using a plain cutter.

3 Dip into paprika, chopped parsley or chopped nuts and arrange attractively on a plate.

1 In a bowl mix the chopped chicken with the chopped spring onions, red pepper and half the Curry Mayonnaise.

# Chicken and Pasta Salad

*This is a delicious way to use up leftover cooked chicken.*

INGREDIENTS

*Serves 4*

225g/8oz/2 cups tri-coloured pasta twists

30ml/2 tbsp pesto sauce

15ml/1 tbsp olive oil

1 beefsteak tomato

12 stoned black olives

225g/8oz/1$^{1}$/$_{2}$ cups cooked French beans

350g/12oz/3 cups cooked chicken, cubed

salt and black pepper

fresh basil, to garnish

1 Cook the pasta in plenty of boiling, salted water until al dente (about 12 minutes or as directed on the packet).

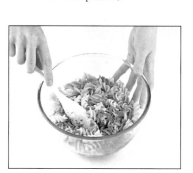

2 Drain the pasta and rinse in plenty of cold running water. Put into a bowl and stir in the pesto sauce and olive oil.

3 Skin the tomato by placing in boiling water for about 10 seconds and then into cold water, to loosen the skin.

4 Cut the tomato into small cubes and add to the pasta with the olives, seasoning and French beans cut into 4cm/1$^{1}$/$_{2}$in lengths. Add the cubed chicken. Toss gently together and transfer to a serving platter. Garnish with fresh basil.

# Mini Spring Rolls

*Use a wok or a large frying pan for this recipe. For a spicier version, sprinkle with a little cayenne pepper.*

INGREDIENTS

*Makes 20*

1 green chilli

120ml/4fl oz/¹/₂ cup vegetable oil

1 small onion, finely chopped

1 clove garlic, crushed

75g/3oz cooked chicken breast

1 small carrot, cut into fine matchsticks

1 spring onion, finely sliced

1 small red pepper, seeded and cut
     into fine matchsticks

25g/1oz beansprouts

15ml/1tbsp sesame oil

4 large sheets filo pastry

egg white, lightly beaten

long chives, to garnish (optional)

45ml/3 tbsp light soy sauce, to serve

1 Carefully remove the seeds from the chilli and chop finely, wearing rubber gloves to protect your hands, if necessary.

2 Heat the wok, then add 30ml/ 2 tbsp of the vegetable oil. When hot, add the onion, garlic and chilli. Stir-fry for 1 minute.

3 Slice the chicken thinly, then add to the wok and fry over a high heat, stirring and tossing constantly until browned.

4 Add the carrot, spring onion and red pepper and stir-fry for 2 minutes. Add the beansprouts, stir in the sesame oil, remove from the heat and leave to cool.

## COOK'S TIP

Always keep filo pastry sheets covered with a damp, clean cloth until needed, to prevent them drying out.

5 Cut each sheet of filo into 5 short strips. Place a small amount of filling at one end of each strip, then fold in the long sides and roll up the pastry. Seal and glaze the parcels with the egg white, then chill, uncovered, for 15 minutes before frying.

6 Wipe out the wok with kitchen paper, heat it, and add the remaining vegetable oil. When the oil is hot, fry the rolls in batches until crisp and golden brown. Drain on kitchen paper and serve dipped in light soy sauce.

# Barbecued Jerk Chicken

*Jerk refers to the blend of herb and spice seasoning rubbed into meat, before it is roasted over charcoal sprinkled with pimiento berries. In Jamaica, jerk seasoning was originally used only for pork, but jerked chicken is equally good.*

### INGREDIENTS

*Serves 4*

8 chicken pieces

*For the marinade*
5ml/1 tsp ground allspice
5ml/1 tsp ground cinnamon
5ml/1 tsp dried thyme
1.5ml/$^{1}/_{4}$ tsp freshly grated nutmeg
10ml/2 tsp demerara sugar
2 garlic cloves, crushed
15ml/1 tbsp finely chopped onion
15ml/1 tbsp chopped spring onion
15ml/1 tbsp vinegar
30ml/2 tbsp oil
15ml/1 tbsp lime juice
1 hot chilli pepper, chopped
salt and black pepper
salad leaves, to serve

1 Combine all the marinade ingredients in a small bowl. Using a fork, mash them together well to form a thick paste.

2 Lay the chicken pieces on a plate or board and make several lengthways slits in the flesh. Rub the seasoning all over the chicken and into the slits.

3 Place the chicken pieces in a dish, cover with clear film and marinate overnight in the fridge. Shake off any excess seasoning from the chicken. Brush with oil and place either on a baking sheet if cooking inside or on a barbecue grill if barbecuing.

4 Cook under a preheated grill for 45 minutes, turning often. Or, if barbecuing, light the coals and when ready, cook over the coals for 30 minutes, turning often. Serve hot with salad leaves.

> COOK'S TIP
>
> The flavour is best if you marinate the chicken overnight.

# Chicken, Bacon and Walnut Terrine

*To seal the terrine in the tin for longer storage, pour on melted lard.*

INGREDIENTS

*Serves 8–10*

2 boneless chicken breasts

1 large garlic clove, crushed

$^{1}/_{2}$ slice bread

1 egg

350g/12oz bacon chops (the fattier the better), minced or finely chopped

225g/8oz chicken or turkey livers, finely chopped

25g/1oz/$^{1}/_{4}$ cup chopped walnuts, toasted

30ml/2 tbsp sweet sherry or Madeira

2.5ml/$^{1}/_{2}$ tsp ground allspice

2.5ml/$^{1}/_{2}$ tsp cayenne pepper

pinch each ground nutmeg and cloves

8 long rashers streaky bacon, rind removed

salt and black pepper

chicory leaves and chives, to garnish

1 Cut the chicken breasts into thin strips and season lightly. Mash the garlic, bread and egg together. Work in the chopped bacon (using your hands is really the best way) and then the finely chopped livers. Stir in the chopped walnuts, sherry or Madeira, spices and seasoning to taste.

2 Preheat the oven to 200°C/400°F/Gas 6. Stretch each of the bacon rashers with a palette knife and use to line a 675g/1$^{1}/_{2}$lb loaf tin, then pack in half of the meat mixture.

3 Lay the chicken strips on the top and spread the rest of the mixture over. Cover the loaf tin with lightly-greased foil, seal well and press down very firmly.

4 Place the terrine in a roasting tin half-full of hot water and bake for 1–1$^{1}/_{2}$ hours, or until firm to the touch. Remove from the oven, place weights on the top and leave to cool completely. Drain off any excess fat or liquid while the terrine is warm.

5 When really cold, turn out the terrine, cut into thick slices and serve at once, garnished with a few chicory leaves and chives.

# Fusilli with Chicken, Tomatoes and Broccoli

*This is a really hearty main-course salad for a hungry family.*

### INGREDIENTS

*Serves 4*

675g/1¹/2lb ripe but firm plum tomatoes, quartered
90ml/6 tbsp olive oil
5ml/1 tsp dried oregano
salt and black pepper
350g/12oz broccoli florets
1 small onion, sliced
5ml/1 tsp dried thyme
450g/1lb/3 cups chicken breast, boned, skinned and cubed
3 garlic cloves, crushed
15ml/1 tbsp fresh lemon juice
450g/1lb fusilli pasta

1 Preheat the oven to 200°C/400°F/Gas 6.

2 Place the tomatoes in a baking dish. Add 15ml/1 tbsp of the oil, the oregano, and 5ml/¹/2 tsp salt and stir to blend.

3 Bake until the tomatoes are just browned, about 30–40 minutes; do not stir.

4 Meanwhile, bring a large pan of salted water to the boil. Add the broccoli and cook until just tender, about 5 minutes. Drain and set aside. (Alternatively, steam the broccoli until tender.)

5 Heat 30ml/2 tbsp of the oil in a large non-stick frying pan. Add the onion, thyme, chicken cubes and 2.5ml/¹/2 tsp salt. Cook over high heat, stirring often, until the meat is cooked and beginning to brown, 5–7 minutes. Add the garlic and cook 1 minute more, stirring.

6 Remove from the heat. Stir in the lemon juice and season with pepper. Keep warm until the pasta is cooked.

7 Bring another large pan of salted water to the boil. Add the fusilli and cook until just tender (check the instructions on the packet for timing). Drain and place in a large bowl. Toss with the remaining oil.

8 Add the broccoli to the chicken mixture. Add to the fusilli. Add the tomatoes and stir gently to blend. Serve immediately.

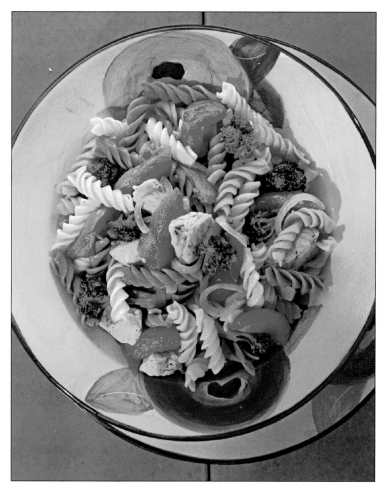

# Chicken Roulades

*These chicken rolls make a light lunch dish for two, or a starter for four. They can be sliced and served cold with a salad.*

INGREDIENTS

*Makes 4*

4 chicken thighs, boned and skinned

115g/4oz chopped fresh or frozen spinach

15g/$^1$/2oz/1 tbsp butter

25g/1oz/2 tbsp pine nuts

pinch of grated nutmeg

25g/1oz/7 tbsp fresh white breadcrumbs

4 rashers rindless streaky bacon

30ml/2 tbsp olive oil

150ml/$^1$/4 pint/$^2$/3 cup white wine
   or chicken stock

10ml/2 tsp cornflour

30ml/2 tbsp single cream

15ml/1 tbsp snipped fresh chives

salt and black pepper

1 Preheat the oven to 180°C/ 350°F/Gas 4. Place the chicken thighs between clear film and flatten with a rolling pin.

2 Put the spinach and butter into a saucepan, heat gently until the spinach has defrosted, if frozen, then increase the heat and cook rapidly, stirring occasionally until all the moisture has been driven off. Add the pine nuts, seasoning, nutmeg and fresh breadcrumbs.

3 Divide the filling between the chicken pieces and roll up neatly. Wrap a rasher of bacon around each piece and tie securely with fine string.

4 Heat the oil in a large frying pan and brown the rolls all over. Lift out using a slotted spoon to drain off the oil and place in a shallow ovenproof dish.

5 Pour over the wine or stock, cover, and bake for 15–20 minutes, or until tender. Transfer the chicken to a serving plate and remove the string. Strain the cooking liquid into a saucepan.

6 Blend the cornflour with a little cold water and add to the juices in the pan, along with the cream. Bring to the boil, stirring until thick. Adjust the seasoning and add the chives. Pour the sauce around the chicken and serve.

# Chicken Liver, Bacon and Tomato Salad

*Warm salads are especially welcome during the autumn months when the evenings are growing shorter and cooler. Try this rich salad with sweet spinach and bitter leaves of frisée lettuce.*

INGREDIENTS

*Serves 4*

225g/8oz young spinach, stems removed

1 frisée lettuce

105ml/7 tbsp groundnut or sunflower oil

175g/6oz rindless unsmoked bacon, cut into strips

75g/3oz day-old bread, crusts removed and cut into short fingers

450g/1lb chicken livers

115g/4oz cherry tomatoes

salt and black pepper

1 Place the salad leaves in a salad bowl. Heat 60ml/4 tbsp of the oil in a large frying pan. Add the bacon and cook for 3–4 minutes or until crisp and brown. Remove the bacon with a slotted spoon and drain on a piece of kitchen paper.

2 To make the croûtons, fry the bread in the bacon-flavoured oil, tossing until crisp and golden. Drain on kitchen paper.

3 Heat the remaining 45ml/3 tbsp of oil in the frying pan, add the chicken livers and fry briskly for 2–3 minutes. Turn out over the salad leaves, add the bacon, croûtons and tomatoes. Season, toss and serve.

# Chicken Liver and Marsala Pâté

*This is a really quick and simple pâté to make, yet it has a delicious – and quite sophisticated – flavour. It contains Marsala, a soft and pungent fortified wine from Sicily. If it is unavailable, use brandy or a medium-dry sherry.*

INGREDIENTS

*Serves 4*

350g/12oz chicken livers,
    defrosted if frozen
225g/8oz/1 cup butter, softened
2 garlic cloves, crushed
15ml/1 tbsp Marsala
5ml/1 tsp chopped fresh sage
salt and black pepper
8 sage leaves, to garnish
thin, crisp toast, to serve

1 Pick over the chicken livers, then rinse and dry with kitchen paper. Melt 25g/1oz/2 tbsp of the butter in a frying pan, and fry the chicken livers with the garlic over a medium heat for about 5 minutes, or until they are firm but still pink in the middle.

2 Transfer the livers to a blender or food processor, using a slotted spoon, and add the Marsala and chopped sage.

3 Melt 150g/5oz/10 tbsp of the remaining butter in the frying pan, stirring to loosen any sediment, then pour into the blender or processor and blend until smooth. Season well.

4 Spoon the pâté into four individual pots and smooth the surface. Melt the remaining butter in a separate pan and pour over the pâtés. Garnish with sage leaves and chill until set. Serve with triangles of toast.

# Wild Rice and Chicken Salad

*Once you have cooked the wild rice,
this is a very simple salad to make.*

INGREDIENTS

*Serves 4*

175g/6oz/1 cup dry weight wild rice,
    boiled or steamed

2 celery sticks, thinly sliced

50g/2oz spring onions, chopped

115g/4oz/1$^{1}/_{2}$ cups small button
    mushrooms, quartered

450g/1lb cooked chicken breast, diced

120ml/4 fl oz/$^{1}/_{2}$ cup vinaigrette dressing

5ml/1 tsp fresh thyme leaves

2 pears, peeled, halved and cored

25g/1oz/$^{1}/_{4}$ cup walnut pieces, toasted

1 Combine the cooked and
cooled wild rice with the celery,
spring onions, mushrooms and
chicken in a large bowl.

2 Add the dressing and thyme;
toss well together.

3 Thinly slice the pear halves
lengthways without cutting
through the stalk end and spread
the slices into a fan. Divide the
salad among 4 plates. Garnish each
with a fanned pear half and
walnuts.

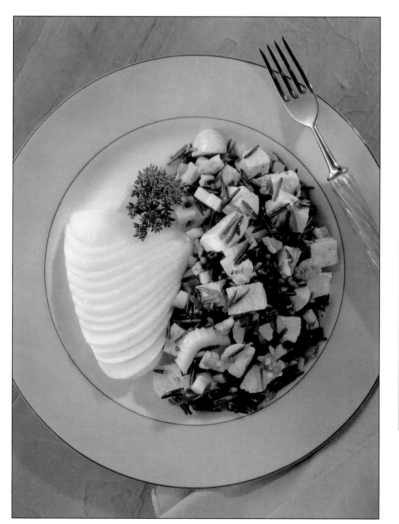

### COOKING WILD RICE

To boil: Add the rice to a large
pot of boiling salted water
(about four parts water to each
one of rice). Bring back to a
gentle boil and cook for 45–50
minutes or until the rice is
tender but still firm and has
begun to split open. Drain well.
To steam: Put the rice in a
saucepan with the measured
quantity of salted water. Bring to
the boil, cover and steam over
very low heat for 45–50 minutes
or until tender. Cook uncovered
for the last 5 minutes to
evaporate excess water.

# Spiced Chicken Livers

*Chicken livers can be bought frozen, but make sure that you defrost them thoroughly before using. Serve as a first course or light meal along with a mixed salad and garlic bread.*

### INGREDIENTS

*Serves 4*

350g/12oz chicken livers

115g/4oz/1 cup plain flour

2.5ml/$\frac{1}{2}$ tsp ground coriander

2.5ml/$\frac{1}{2}$ tsp ground cumin

2.5ml/$\frac{1}{2}$ tsp ground cardamom
   seeds

1.5ml/$\frac{1}{4}$ tsp ground paprika

1.5ml/$\frac{1}{4}$ tsp ground nutmeg

90ml/6 tbsp olive oil

salt and black pepper

1 Dry the chicken livers on kitchen paper, removing any unwanted pieces. Cut the large livers in half and leave the smaller ones whole.

2 Mix the flour with all the spices and the seasoning.

3 Coat a few of the livers with spiced flour, separating each piece. Heat the oil in a large frying pan and fry the livers in small batches. (This helps to keep the oil temperature high and prevents the flour from becoming soggy.)

4 Fry quickly, stirring frequently, until crispy. Keep warm and repeat with the remaining livers. Serve immediately with warm garlic bread and salad.

# Grilled Chicken Salad with Lavender

*Lavender may seem like an odd salad ingredient, but its delightful scent has a natural affinity with sweet garlic, orange and other wild herbs. A serving of polenta makes this salad both filling and delicious.*

INGREDIENTS

*Serves 4*

4 chicken breasts, boned

900ml/1¹/2 pints/3³/4 cups light chicken
    stock

175g/6oz/1 cup fine polenta

50g/2oz/4tbsp butter

450g/1lb young spinach

175g/6oz lamb's lettuce

8 sprigs fresh lavender

8 small tomatoes, halved

salt and black pepper

*Lavender Marinade*

6 fresh lavender flowers

10ml/2 tsp finely grated orange rind

2 cloves garlic, crushed

10ml/2 tsp clear honey

salt

30ml/2 tbsp olive oil

10ml/2 tsp chopped fresh thyme

10ml/2 tsp chopped fresh marjoram

1 To make the marinade, strip the lavender flowers from the stems and combine with the orange rind, garlic, honey and salt. Add the olive oil and herbs. Slash the chicken deeply, spread the mixture over the chicken and leave to marinate in a cool place for at least 20 minutes.

2 To cook the polenta, bring the chicken stock to the boil in a heavy saucepan. Add the polenta in a steady stream, stirring all the time until thick: this will take 2–3 minutes. Turn the cooked polenta out on to a 2.5cm/1in deep buttered tray and allow to cool.

3 Heat the grill to a moderate temperature. (If using a barbecue, let the embers settle to a steady glow.) Grill the chicken for about 15 minutes, turning once.

4 Cut the polenta into 2.5cm/1in cubes with a wet knife. Heat the butter in a large frying pan and fry the polenta until golden.

5 Wash the salad leaves and spin dry, then divide among 4 large plates. Slice each chicken breast and lay over the salad. Place the polenta among the salad, decorate with sprigs of lavender and tomatoes, season and serve.

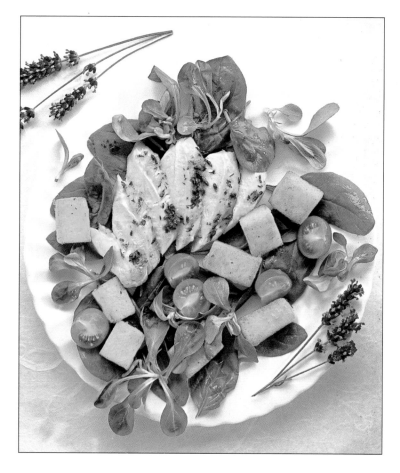

# Chicken Liver Pâté

*A deliciously smooth pâté which is ideal to spread on hot toast.*

*Serves 6 or more*

50g/2oz/4 tbsp butter

1 onion, finely chopped

350g/12oz chicken livers, trimmed of all dark or greenish parts

60ml/4 tbsp medium sherry

25g/1oz full-fat soft cheese

15–30ml/1–2 tbsp lemon juice

2 hard-boiled eggs, chopped

salt and pepper

50–75g/2–3oz/$^1$/4 cup clarified butter

1 Melt the butter in a frying pan. Add the onion and livers and cook until the onion is soft and the livers are lightly browned and no longer pink in the centre.

2 Add the sherry and boil until reduced by half. Cool slightly.

---

### COOK'S TIP

Add brandy instead of sherry for a special occasion dinner party.

---

3 Turn the mixture into a food processor or blender and add the soft cheese and 1 tablespoon lemon juice. Blend until smooth.

4 Add the hard-boiled eggs and blend briefly. Season with salt and pepper. Taste and add more lemon juice if liked.

5 Pack the liver pâté into a mould or into individual ramekins. Smooth the surface.

6 Spoon a layer of clarified butter over the surface of the pâté. Chill until firm. Serve at room temperature, with hot toast or savoury biscuits.

# Maryland Salad

*Barbecue-grilled chicken, sweetcorn, bacon, banana and watercress combine here in a sensational main-course salad. Serve with jacket potatoes and a knob of butter.*

INGREDIENTS

*Serves 4*

4 chicken breasts, boned

225g/8oz rindless unsmoked bacon

4 corn on the cob

45ml/3 tbsp butter, softened

4 ripe bananas, peeled and halved

4 firm tomatoes, halved

1 escarole or butterhead lettuce

1 bunch watercress

salt and black pepper

*For the dressing*

75ml/5 tbsp groundnut oil

15ml/1 tbsp white wine vinegar

10ml/2 tsp maple syrup

10ml/2 tsp mild mustard

1 Season the chicken breasts, brush with oil and barbecue or grill for 15 minutes, turning once. Barbecue or grill the bacon for 8–10 minutes, or until crisp.

2 Bring a large saucepan of salted water to the boil. Shuck and trim the corn cobs. Boil for 20 minutes. For extra flavour, brush with butter and brown over the barbecue or under the grill. Barbecue or grill the bananas and tomatoes for 6–8 minutes, brush these with butter too if you wish.

3 To make the dressing, combine the oil, vinegar, maple syrup and mustard with seasoning and 15ml/1 tbsp water in a screw-top jar and shake well.

4 Wash, spin thoroughly and dress the salad leaves.

5 Distribute the salad leaves among 4 large plates. Slice the chicken and arrange over the leaves with the bacon, banana, sweetcorn and tomatoes.

# Corn-fed Chicken Salad

*A light first course for eight or a
substantial main course for four.*

*Serves 8*

1.75kg/4lb corn-fed chicken

300ml/$^1$/2 pint/1$^1$/4 cups white wine
   and water, mixed

24 x 5mm/$^1$/4 in slices French bread

1 garlic clove, peeled

225g/8oz French beans, trimmed and cut
   in 5cm/2in lengths

115g/4oz fresh young spinach leaves,
   washed and torn into small pieces

2 sticks celery, thinly sliced

2 sun-dried tomatoes, chopped

2 spring onions, thinly sliced

fresh chives and parsley, to garnish

*For the vinaigrette*

30ml/2 tbsp red wine vinegar

90ml/6 tbsp olive oil

15ml/1 tbsp wholegrain mustard

15ml/1 tbsp clear honey

30ml/2 tbsp chopped mixed fresh herbs

10ml/2 tsp finely chopped capers

salt and black pepper

2 Put all the ingredients for the
vinaigrette into a screw-topped
jar and shake vigorously. Adjust
the seasoning to taste.

3 Toast the French bread until
golden brown. Rub with garlic.

4 Cook the French beans in
boiling water until just tender.
Drain and rinse under cold water.

5 Arrange the spinach on serving
plates with the celery, French
beans, sun-dried tomatoes,
chicken and spring onions. Spoon
over the dressing, add the toasted
croûtes and garnish with chives
and parsley.

1 Preheat the oven to 190°C/
375°F/Gas 5. Put the chicken,
wine and water into a casserole.
Roast for 1$^1$/2 hours until tender.
Leave to cool in the liquid. Remove
the skin and bones and cut the
flesh into small pieces.

# Grilled Chicken with Pica de Gallo Salsa

This dish originates from Mexico. Its hot fruity flavours form the essence of Tex-Mex cooking.

## INGREDIENTS

*Serves 4*

4 chicken breasts

pinch of celery salt and cayenne pepper
    combined

30ml/2 tbsp vegetable oil

corn chips, to serve

*For the salsa*

275g/10oz watermelon

175g/6oz canteloupe melon

1 small red onion

1–2 green chillies

30ml/2 tbsp lime juice

60ml/4 tbsp chopped fresh coriander

pinch of salt

1 Preheat a moderate grill. Slash the chicken breasts deeply to speed up the cooking time.

2 Season the chicken with celery salt and cayenne, brush with oil and grill for about 15 minutes.

3 To make the salsa, remove the rind and as many seeds as you can from the melons. Finely dice the flesh and put it into a bowl.

4 Finely chop the onion, split the chillies (discarding the seeds which contain most of the heat) and chop. Take care when handling cut chillies. Mix with the melon.

5 Add the lime juice and coriander, and season with salt. Turn the salsa into a small bowl.

6 Arrange the grilled chicken on a plate and serve with the salsa and a handful of corn chips.

### COOK'S TIP

To capture the spirit of Tex-Mex food, cook the chicken over a barbecue and eat shaded from the hot summer sun.

# Chicken Goujons

*Serve as a first course for eight people or as a filling main course for four. Delicious served with new baby potatoes and a green salad.*

INGREDIENTS

*Serves 8*

4 boned and skinned chicken breasts

175g/6oz/3 cups fresh breadcrumbs

5ml/1 tsp ground coriander

10ml/2 tsp ground paprika

2.5ml/$\frac{1}{2}$ tsp ground cumin

45ml/3 tbsp plain flour

2 eggs, beaten

oil, for deep-frying

salt and black pepper

lemon slices, to garnish

sprigs of fresh coriander, to garnish

*For the dip*

300ml/$\frac{1}{2}$ pint/1$\frac{1}{4}$ cups Greek yogurt

30ml/2 tbsp lemon juice

60ml/4 tbsp chopped fresh coriander

60ml/4 tbsp chopped fresh parsley

1 Divide the chicken breasts into two natural fillets. Place them between two sheets of clear film and using a rolling pin, flatten each one to a thickness of 1cm/$\frac{1}{2}$ in.

2 Cut the chicken into diagonal 2.5cm/1in strips.

3 Mix the breadcrumbs with the spices and seasoning. Toss the chicken fillet pieces (goujons) into the flour, keeping them separate.

4 Dip the goujons into the beaten egg and then coat in the breadcrumb mixture.

5 Thoroughly mix all the ingredients for the dip together and season to taste. Cover and chill until required.

6 Heat the oil in a heavy-based pan. It is ready for deep-frying when a piece of bread tossed into the oil sizzles on the surface. Fry the goujons in batches until golden and crisp. Drain on kitchen paper and keep warm in the oven until all the chicken has been fried. Garnish with lemon slices and sprigs of fresh coriander and serve with the yogurt dip.

# Coronation Chicken

*A summary favourite – serve with a crisp green salad.*

INGREDIENTS

*Serves 8*

$^1/_2$ lemon

2.25kg/5–5$^1/_4$lb chicken

1 onion, quartered

1 carrot, quartered

large bouquet garni

8 black peppercorns, crushed

salt

watercress sprigs, to garnish

*For the sauce*

1 small onion, chopped

15g/$^1/_2$oz/1 tbsp butter

15ml/1 tbsp curry paste

15ml/1 tbsp tomato purée

120ml/4fl oz/$^1/_2$ cup red wine

bay leaf

juice of $^1/_2$ lemon, or more to taste

10–15ml/2–3 tsp apricot jam

300ml/$^1/_2$ pint/1$^1/_4$ cups mayonnaise

120ml/4fl oz/$^1/_2$ cup whipping cream,
   whipped

salt and black pepper

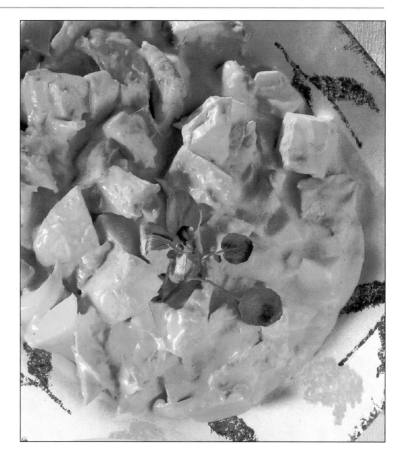

1 Put the lemon half in the chicken cavity, then place the chicken in a saucepan that it just fits. Add the vegetables, bouquet garni, peppercorns and salt.

2 Add sufficient water to come two-thirds of the way up the chicken, bring to the boil, then cover and cook gently for 1$^1/_2$ hours, until the juices run clear.

3 Transfer the chicken to a large bowl, pour over the cooking liquid and leave to cool. Skin, bone, then chop the chicken flesh.

4 To make the sauce, cook the onion in the butter until soft. Add the curry paste, tomato purée, wine, bay leaf and lemon juice, then cook for 10 minutes. Add the apricot jam; sieve and cool.

5 Beat the sauce into the mayonnaise. Fold in the cream; add seasoning, then stir in the chicken and garnish with watercress.

# Smoked Chicken and Lentil Soup

*Smoked chicken gives added depth of flavour to this hearty soup.*

INGREDIENTS

*Serves 4*

25g/1oz/2 tbsp butter

1 large carrot, chopped

1 onion, chopped

1 celery stick, chopped

1 leek, white part only, chopped

115g/4oz/1$^1$/$_2$ cups mushrooms, chopped

50ml/2fl oz/$^1$/$_4$ cup dry white wine

1 litre/1$^3$/$_4$ pints/4 cups chicken stock

10ml/2 tsp dried thyme

1 bay leaf

120ml/4fl oz/$^1$/$_2$ cup lentils

225g/8oz/1$^1$/$_2$ cups smoked
   chicken meat, diced

salt and pepper

chopped fresh parsley, to garnish

1 Melt the butter in a large saucepan. Add the carrot, onion, celery, leek and mushrooms. Cook gently until golden, about 3–5 minutes.

2 Stir in the wine and chicken stock. Bring to the boil and skim any foam that rises to the surface. Add the thyme and bay leaf. Lower the heat, cover, and simmer gently for 30 minutes.

3 Add the lentils and continue cooking, covered, until they are just tender, 30–40 minutes more. Stir the soup from time to time.

4 Stir in the chicken and season to taste. Cook until just heated through. Ladle into bowls and garnish with chopped parsley.

# Peanut Chicken in Pineapple Boats

*An impressive looking dish to serve at a dinner party.*

*Serves 4*

2 small ripe pineapples

225g/8 oz/1¹/₂ cups cooked chicken
    breast, cut into bite-size pieces

2 celery sticks, diced

50g/2oz spring onions, white and green
    parts, chopped

225g/8oz seedless green grapes

40g/1¹/₂ oz salted peanuts, coarsely
    chopped

*Dressing*

75g/3oz smooth peanut butter

120ml/4 fl oz/¹/₂ cup mayonnaise

30ml/2 tbsp cream or milk

1 garlic clove, finely chopped

5ml/1 tsp mild curry powder

15ml/1tbsp apricot jam

salt and black pepper

1 Make 4 pineapple boats from the pineapples. Cut the flesh removed from the boats into bite-size pieces.

2 Combine the pineapple flesh, chicken, celery, spring onions and grapes in a bowl.

3 Put all the dressing ingredients in another bowl and mix with a wooden spoon or whisk until evenly blended. Season with salt and pepper. (The dressing will be thick, but will be thinned by the juices from the pineapple.)

4 Add the dressing to the pineapple and chicken mixture. Fold together gently but thoroughly.

5 Divide the chicken salad among the pineapple boats. Sprinkle the peanuts over the top before serving.

# Spicy Sweetcorn Soup

*This is a very quick and easy soup,
made in minutes. If you are using
frozen prawns, then defrost them
first before adding to the soup.*

INGREDIENTS

*Serves 4*

2.5ml/¹/₂ tsp sesame or sunflower oil

2 spring onions, thinly sliced

1 garlic clove, crushed

600ml/1 pint/2¹/₂ cups chicken stock

425g/15oz can cream-style sweetcorn

225g/8oz/1¹/₄ cups cooked, peeled prawns

5ml/1 tsp green chilli paste or
    chilli sauce (optional)

salt and black pepper

fresh coriander leaves, to garnish

1 Heat the oil in a large heavy-
based saucepan and sauté the
spring onions and garlic over a
medium heat for 1 minute, until
softened, but not browned.

### COOK'S TIP

If cream-style corn is not
available, use ordinary canned
sweetcorn, puréed in a food
processor for just a few seconds,
until creamy yet with some
texture left.

2 Stir in the chicken stock,
cream-style sweetcorn, prawns
and chilli paste or sauce, if using.

3 Bring the soup to the boil,
stirring occasionally. Season to
taste, then serve at once, sprinkled
with fresh coriander leaves.

# Warm Chicken and Coriander Salad

*This salad needs to be served warm to make the most of the wonderful sesame and coriander flavourings. It makes a simple starter or a delicious light lunch dish.*

INGREDIENTS

*Serves 6*

4 medium chicken breasts, boned and
   skinned

225g/8oz mange-touts

2 heads decorative lettuce such as lollo
   rosso or oakleaf

3 carrots, peeled and cut into small
   matchsticks

175g/6oz/2$^3$/4 cups button mushrooms,
   sliced

6 rashers of bacon, fried and chopped

1 tbsp chopped fresh coriander leaves,
   to garnish

*Dressing*

120ml/4fl oz/$^1$/2 cup lemon juice

30ml/2 tbsp wholegrain mustard

250ml/8fl oz/1 cup olive oil

60ml/4 tbsp sesame oil

1 tsp coriander seeds, crushed

1 Mix all the dressing ingredients in a bowl. Place the chicken breasts in a shallow dish and pour on half the dressing. Chill overnight, and store the remaining dressing in the fridge.

2 Cook the mange-touts for 2 minutes in boiling water, then cool under running cold water to stop them cooking any further. Tear the lettuces into small pieces and mix the other salad ingredients and the bacon together. Arrange all these in individual serving dishes.

3 Grill the chicken breasts until cooked through, then slice them on the diagonal into quite thin pieces. Divide among the bowls of salad, and add some dressing to each dish. Combine quickly and scatter some fresh coriander over each bowl.

# Beetroot and Apricot Swirl

*This soup is most attractive if you swirl together the two coloured mixtures, but if you prefer they can be mixed together to save on time and washing up.*

### INGREDIENTS

Serves 4

4 large cooked beetroot, roughly
   chopped
1 small onion, roughly chopped
600ml/1 pint/2¹/₂ cups chicken stock
200g/7oz/1 cup ready-to-eat
   dried apricots
250ml/8fl oz/1 cup orange juice
salt and black pepper

1 Place the beetroot and half the onion in a pan with the stock. Bring to the boil, then reduce the heat, cover and simmer for about 10 minutes. Purée in a food processor or blender.

2 Place the rest of the onion in a saucepan with the apricots and orange juice, cover and simmer gently for about 15 minutes, until tender. Process to a purée in a food processor or blender.

3 Return the two mixtures to the saucepans and reheat. Season to taste with salt and pepper, then swirl them together in individual soup bowls for a marbled effect.

## COOK'S TIP

The apricot mixture should be the same consistency as the beetroot mixture – if it is too thick, then add a little more orange juice.

# Sweet and Sour Kebabs

*This marinade contains sugar and will burn very easily, so grill the kebabs slowly, turning often. Serve with Harlequin Rice.*

INGREDIENTS

*Serves 4*

2 chicken breasts, boned and skinned

8 pickling onions or 2 medium onions, peeled

4 rindless streaky bacon rashers

3 firm bananas

1 red pepper, seeded and sliced

*For the marinade*

30ml/2 tbsp soft brown sugar

15ml/1 tbsp Worcestershire sauce

30ml/2 tbsp lemon juice

salt and black pepper

*For the Harlequin Rice*

30ml/2 tbsp olive oil

225g/8oz/generous 1 cup cooked rice

115g/4oz/1 cup cooked peas

1 small red pepper, seeded and diced

1 Mix together the marinade ingredients. Cut each chicken breast into four pieces, add to the marinade, cover and leave for at least 4 hours or preferably overnight in the fridge.

2 Peel the pickling onions, blanch them in boiling water for 5 minutes and drain. If using medium onions, quarter them after blanching.

3 Cut each rasher of bacon in half. Peel the bananas and cut each into three pieces. Wrap a rasher of bacon around each piece of banana.

4 Thread on to metal skewers with the chicken pieces, onions and pepper slices. Brush with the marinade.

5 Grill or barbecue over low coals for 15 minutes, turning and basting frequently with the marinade. Keep warm while you prepare the rice.

6 Heat the oil in a frying pan and add the rice, peas and diced pepper. Stir until heated through and serve with the kebabs.

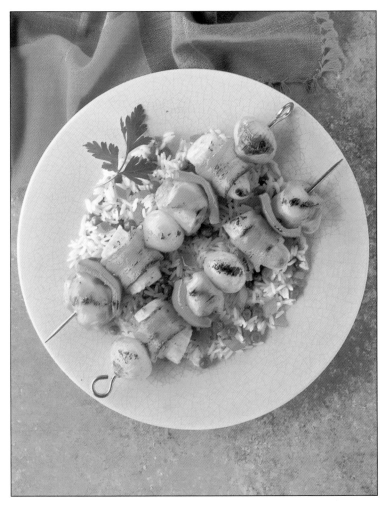

# Red Pepper Soup with Lime

*The beautiful rich red colour of this soup makes it a very attractive starter or light lunch. For a special dinner, toast some tiny croûtons and serve sprinkled on to the soup.*

INGREDIENTS

*Serves 4–6*

4 red peppers, seeded and chopped

1 large onion, chopped

5ml/1 tsp olive oil

1 garlic clove, crushed

1 small red chilli, sliced

45ml/3 tbsp tomato purée

900ml/1$^1$/$_2$ pints/3$^3$/$_4$ cups chicken stock

finely grated rind and juice of 1 lime

salt and black pepper

shreds of lime rind, to garnish

1 Cook the chopped peppers and onion gently in the oil in a covered saucepan for about 5 minutes until softened, shaking the pan occasionally.

2 Stir in the garlic, then add the chilli with the tomato purée. Stir in half the stock, then bring to the boil. Cover the pan and simmer for 10 minutes.

3 Cool slightly, then purée in a food processor or blender. Return to the pan, then add the remaining stock, the lime rind and juice, and seasoning.

4 Bring the soup back to the boil, then serve at once with a few strips of lime rind, scattered into each bowl.

# Chicken and Fruit Salad

*The chickens may be cooked a day before eating and the salad can be quickly put together for lunch.*

INGREDIENTS

*Serves 8*

4 sprigs tarragon or rosemary

2 x 1.75kg/4lb chickens

65g/2$^1$/2oz/5 tbsp softened butter

150ml/$^1$/4 pint/$^2$/3 cup chicken stock

150ml/$^1$/4 pint/$^2$/3 cup white wine

115g/4oz/1 cup walnut pieces

1 small cantaloupe melon

lettuce leaves

450g/1lb seedless grapes or stoned
   cherries

salt and black pepper

*Dressing*

30ml/2 tbsp tarragon vinegar

120ml/4 fl oz/$^1$/2 cup light olive oil

30ml/2 tbsp chopped mixed fresh herbs,
   e.g. parsley, mint and tarragon

1 Preheat the oven to 200°C/400°F/Gas 6. Put the herb sprigs inside the chickens and season. Tie the chickens with string. Spread the chickens with 50g/2oz/4 tbsp of the softened butter, place in a roasting tin and pour round the stock. Cover loosely with foil and roast for about 1$^1$/2 hours, basting twice, until browned and the juices run clear. Remove the chickens from the roasting tin.

2 Add the wine to the roasting tin. Bring to the boil and cook until syrupy. Strain and leave to cool. Heat the remaining butter in a frying pan and gently fry the walnuts until browned. Drain and cool. Scoop the melon into balls or into cubes, joint the chickens.

3 To make the dressing, whisk the vinegar and oil together with a little salt and freshly ground black pepper. Remove all the fat from the chicken juices and add these to the dressing with the herbs. Adjust the seasoning.

4 Arrange the chicken pieces on a bed of lettuce, scatter over the grapes or stoned cherries, melon balls or cubes and spoon over the herb dressing. Sprinkle with toasted walnuts.

# Leek, Potato and Rocket Soup

*Rocket, with its distinctive, peppery taste, is wonderful in this deliciously filling soup. Serve it hot with ciabatta croûtons.*

### INGREDIENTS

*Serves 4–6*

50g/2oz/4 tbsp butter

1 onion, chopped

3 leeks, chopped

2 potatoes, diced

900ml/1$^1$/$_2$ pints/3$^3$/$_4$ cups light
   chicken stock

2 large handfuls rocket, roughly
   chopped

150ml/$^1$/$_4$ pint/$^2$/$_3$ cup double cream

salt and black pepper

garlic-flavoured croûtons, to serve

1 Melt the butter in a large heavy-based pan, add the onion, leeks and potatoes and stir until the vegetables are coated.

2 Cover and leave the vegetables to sweat for about 15 minutes. Pour in the stock, cover once again, then simmer the vegetables for 20 minutes, until tender.

3 Press the soup through a sieve or food mill and return to the rinsed-out pan. (When puréeing the soup, don't use a blender or food processor, as these will give the soup a gluey texture.) Add the chopped rocket and cook gently for 5 minutes.

4 Stir in the cream, then season to taste and reheat gently. Ladle the soup into warm soup bowls and serve with the garlic-flavoured croûtons.

# Warm Stir-fried Salad

Warm salads are becoming increasingly popular because they are delicious and nutritious. Arrange the salad leaves on four individual plates, so the hot stir-fry can be served straight from the wok, ensuring the lettuce remains crisp and the chicken warm.

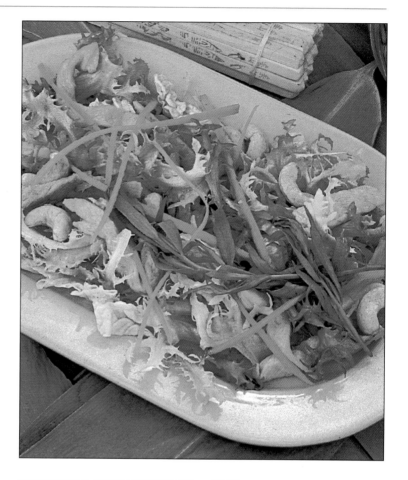

## INGREDIENTS

Serves 4

15ml/1 tbsp fresh tarragon

2 chicken breasts, about 225g/8oz each, boned and skinned

5cm/2in piece fresh root ginger, peeled and finely chopped

45ml/3 tbsp light soy sauce

15ml/1 tbsp sugar

15ml/1 tbsp sunflower oil

1 head Chinese lettuce

1/2 frisée lettuce, torn into bite-size pieces

115g/4oz/1 cup unsalted cashew nuts

2 large carrots, peeled and cut into fine strips

salt and black pepper

1 Chop the fresh tarragon. Cut the chicken into fine strips and place in a bowl.

2 To make the marinade, mix together in a bowl the tarragon, ginger, soy sauce, sugar and seasoning.

3 Pour the marinade over the chicken strips and leave to marinate for 2–4 hours.

4 Strain the chicken from the marinade, reserving the liquid. Heat a wok or large frying pan, then add the oil. When the oil is hot, stir-fry the chicken for 3 minutes, add the marinade and bubble for 2–3 minutes.

5 Slice the Chinese lettuce and arrange on a plate with the frisée. Toss the cashews and carrots together with the chicken and sauce, pile on top of the bed of lettuce and serve immediately.

# Carrot and Coriander Soup

*Use a good home-made stock for this soup – it adds a far greater depth of flavour than stock made from cubes.*

## INGREDIENTS

*Serves 4*

50g/2oz/4 tbsp butter

3 leeks, sliced

450g/1lb carrots, sliced

15ml/1 tbsp ground coriander

1.2 litres/2 pints/5 cups chicken stock

150ml/¼ pint/⅔ cup Greek-style yogurt

salt and black pepper

30–45ml/2–3 tbsp chopped fresh coriander, to garnish

1 Melt the butter in a large pan. Add the leeks and carrots and stir well to coat with the butter. Cover and cook for about 10 minutes, until the vegetables are beginning to soften but not colour.

2 Stir in the ground coriander and cook for about 1 minute. Pour in the stock and season to taste. Bring to the boil, cover and simmer for about 20 minutes, until the leeks and carrots are tender.

3 Leave to cool slightly, then purée the soup in a blender until smooth. Return the soup to the pan and add 30ml/2 tbsp of the yogurt, then taste the soup and adjust the seasoning. Reheat gently but do not boil.

4 Ladle the soup into bowls and add a spoonful of yogurt to the centre of each. Scatter over the coriander and serve immediately.

# HOT & SPICY

~

# Green Pea and Mint Soup

*This soup is equally delicious cold. Instead of reheating it after puréeing, leave it to cool and then chill lightly in the fridge. Stir in the swirl of cream just before serving.*

INGREDIENTS

*Serves 4*

50g/2oz/4 tbsp butter

4 spring onions, chopped

450g/1lb/4 cups fresh or frozen peas

600ml/1 pint/2$^1$/$_2$ cups chicken
   stock

2 large mint sprigs

600ml/1 pint/2$^1$/$_2$ cups milk

pinch of sugar (optional)

salt and pepper

single cream, to serve

small mint sprigs, to garnish

1 Heat the butter in a large saucepan, add the spring onions, and cook gently until softened but not coloured.

### FREEZER NOTE

The soup can be frozen for up to two months after step 2. Allow it to thaw in the fridge before puréeing and reheating.

2 Stir the peas into the pan, add the stock and mint and bring to the boil. Cover and simmer very gently for about 30 minutes for fresh peas or 15 minutes if you are using frozen peas, until the peas are very tender. Remove about 45ml/3 tbsp of the peas using a slotted spoon, and put to one side for the garnish.

3 Pour the soup into a food processor or blender, add the milk and purée until smooth. Then return the soup to the pan and reheat gently. Season to taste, adding a pinch of sugar, if liked.

4 Pour the soup into individual bowls. Swirl a little cream into each, then garnish with mint and the reserved peas.

# Chicken Biryani

*A deceptively easy curry to make, and very tasty, too.*

*Serves 4*

275g/10oz/1$^1$/2 cups basmati rice, rinsed

2.5ml/$^1$/2 tsp salt

5 whole cardamom pods

2–3 whole cloves

1 cinnamon stick

45ml/3 tbsp vegetable oil

3 onions, sliced

675g/1$^1$/2lb chicken (4 x 175g/6oz chicken
    breasts), cubed, skinned and boned

1.5ml/$^1$/4 tsp ground cloves

5 cardamom pods, seeds removed and
    ground

1.5ml/$^1$/4 tsp hot chilli powder

5ml/1 tsp ground cumin

5ml/1 tsp ground coriander

2.5ml/$^1$/2 tsp black pepper

3 garlic cloves, finely chopped

5ml/1 tsp finely chopped fresh root ginger

juice of 1 lemon

4 tomatoes, sliced

30ml/2 tbsp chopped fresh coriander

150ml/$^1$/4 pint/$^2$/3 cup natural yogurt

2.5ml/$^1$/2 tsp saffron strands soaked in
    10ml/2 tsp hot milk

45ml/3 tbsp toasted flaked almonds and
    fresh coriander sprigs, to garnish

natural yogurt, to serve

1 Preheat the oven to 190°C/
375°F/Gas 5. Bring a pan of
water to the boil and add the rice,
salt, cardamom pods, cloves and
cinnamon stick. Boil for 2 minutes
and then drain, leaving the whole
spices in the rice.

2 Heat the oil in a pan and fry
the onions for 8 minutes, until
browned. Add the chicken
followed by all the ground spices,
the garlic, ginger and lemon juice.
Stir-fry for 5 minutes.

3 Transfer the chicken mixture to
a casserole and lay the sliced
tomatoes on top. Sprinkle over the
fresh coriander, spoon over the
natural yogurt and top with the
drained rice.

4 Drizzle the saffron and milk
over the rice and pour over
150ml/$^1$/4 pint/$^2$/3 cup of water.

5 Cover tightly and bake in the
oven for 1 hour. Transfer to a
warmed serving platter and
remove the whole spices from the
rice. Garnish with toasted almonds
and fresh coriander and serve with
extra natural yogurt.

# New England Spiced Pumpkin Soup

*Pumpkin soup cooked with spices,
brown sugar and orange juice.*

INGREDIENTS

*Serves 4*

25g/1oz/2 tbsp butter

1 onion, finely chopped

1 small garlic clove, crushed

15ml/1 tbsp plain flour

pinch of grated nutmeg

2.5ml/$^1$/$_2$ tsp ground cinnamon

350g/12oz/3 cups pumpkin, seeded,
    peeled and cubed

600ml/1 pint/2$^1$/$_2$ cups chicken stock

150ml/$^1$/$_4$ pint/$^2$/$_3$ cup orange juice

5ml/1 tsp brown sugar

15ml/1 tbsp vegetable oil

2 slices Granary bread without crusts

30ml/2 tbsp sunflower seeds

salt and black pepper

1 Heat the butter in a large
saucepan, add the onion and
garlic and fry gently for 4–5
minutes, until softened. Stir in
the flour, all the spices and the
pumpkin.

2 Cover and cook gently for
about 6 minutes, stirring
occasionally.

3 Pour in the chicken stock and
orange juice and add the
brown sugar. Cover and bring to
the boil, then reduce the heat and
simmer for 20 minutes, until the
pumpkin has softened.

4 Pour half of the mixture into a
blender or food processor and
process until smooth. Return the
soup to the pan with the
remaining chunky mixture. Season
well and heat through, stirring.

5 Meanwhile, make the croûtons.
Heat the oil in a frying pan, cut
the bread into cubes and fry gently
until just beginning to brown. Add
the sunflower seeds and fry for 1–2
minutes. Drain the croûtons and
sunflower seeds on kitchen paper.

6 Serve the soup hot with a few
of the croûtons and sunflower
seeds scattered over the top. Serve
the rest separately.

# Simple Curried Chicken

*A tasty curry that needs very little preparation.*

*Serves 4*

30ml/2 tbsp vegetable oil

1 onion, chopped

1 green or red pepper, seeded and diced

1 garlic clove, finely chopped

25ml/1$^1$/2 tbsp curry powder

2.5ml/$^1$/2 tsp dried thyme

450g/1lb tomatoes, skinned, seeded and chopped, or canned chopped tomatoes

30ml/2 tbsp lemon juice

120ml/4fl oz/$^1$/2 cup water

50g/2oz currants or raisins

salt and black pepper

1.5kg/3–3$^1$/2lb chicken, skinned and cut into 8 pieces

cooked rice, to serve

1 Preheat the oven to 180°C/ 350°F/Gas 4. Heat the vegetable oil in a wide, deep frying pan that has a lid and an ovenproof handle or in a flameproof casserole. Add the chopped onion, diced green or red pepper and garlic. Cook, stirring occasionally, until the vegetables are soft but not too brown.

2 Stir in the curry powder and thyme, then add the tomatoes, lemon juice and water. Bring the sauce to the boil, stirring frequently. Stir in the currants or raisins. Season to taste with salt and pepper.

3 Put the chicken pieces in the frying pan or casserole, arranging them in one layer. Turn to coat them with the sauce. Cover the pan and transfer to the oven. Cook for about 40 minutes or until the chicken is tender. Turn the pieces halfway through cooking.

4 Remove the chicken and sauce to a warmed serving platter. Serve with freshly boiled rice.

### VARIATION

For Curried Chicken Casserole, omit the diced pepper and cook 25ml/1$^1$/2 tbsp finely chopped fresh ginger and 1 green chilli, seeded and finely chopped, with the onion and garlic in a flameproof casserole. In step 3, stir in the curry powder with 450ml/$^3$/4 pint/1$^3$/4 cups natural yogurt; omit the tomatoes, lemon juice and water. Add the chicken pieces, cover and cook in the oven at a lower temperature of 160°C/325°F/Gas 3 for 1–1$^1$/4 hours.

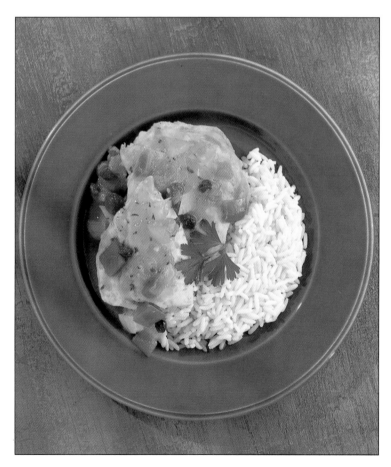

# Thai Chicken Soup

*This filling and tasty soup is very quick to prepare and cook.*

INGREDIENTS

*Serves 4*

15ml/1 tbsp vegetable oil

1 garlic clove, finely chopped

2 boned chicken breasts, about 175g/6oz
each, skinned and chopped

2.5ml/$^1/_2$ tsp ground turmeric

1.5ml/$^1/_4$ tsp hot chilli powder

75g/3oz creamed coconut

900ml/1$^1/_2$ pints/3$^3/_4$ cups hot
chicken stock

30ml/2 tbsp lemon or lime juice

30ml/2 tbsp crunchy peanut butter

50g/2oz/1 cup thread egg noodles, broken
into small pieces

15ml/1 tbsp spring onions, finely chopped

15ml/1 tbsp chopped fresh coriander

salt and black pepper

30ml/2 tbsp desiccated coconut and $^1/_2$
fresh red chilli, seeded and finely
chopped, to garnish

1 Heat the oil in a large pan and fry the garlic for 1 minute until lightly golden. Add the chicken and spices and stir-fry for a further 3–4 minutes.

2 Crumble the creamed coconut into the hot chicken stock and stir until dissolved. Pour on to the chicken and add the lemon juice, peanut butter and egg noodles.

3 Cover the pan and simmer for about 15 minutes.

4 Add the spring onions and fresh coriander, then season well and cook for a further 5 minutes. Meanwhile, place the desiccated coconut and chilli in a small frying pan and heat for 2–3 minutes, stirring frequently.

5 Serve the soup in bowls and sprinkle each one with some fried coconut and chilli.

# Sour Chicken

*There are few cookery concepts that are better suited to today's busy lifestyle than the all-in-one stir-fry. This one has a South-east Asian influence.*

### INGREDIENTS

*Serves 4*

275g/10oz Chinese egg noodles

30ml/2 tbsp vegetable oil

3 spring onions, chopped

1 garlic clove, crushed

2.5cm/1in piece fresh root ginger, peeled and grated

5ml/1 tsp hot paprika

5ml/1 tsp ground coriander

3 chicken breasts, boned and sliced

115g/4oz/1 cup sugar-snap peas, topped and tailed

115g/4oz baby corn on the cob, halved

225g/8oz fresh beansprouts

15ml/1 tbsp cornflour

45ml/3 tbsp soy sauce

45ml/3 tbsp lemon juice

15ml/1 tbsp sugar

45ml/3 tbsp chopped fresh coriander or spring onion tops, to garnish

1 Bring a large saucepan of salted water to the boil. Add the noodles and cook according to the instructions on the packet. Drain, cover and keep warm.

2 Heat the oil. Add the spring onions and cook over a gentle heat. Mix in the next five ingredients, then stir-fry for 3–4 minutes. Add the next three ingredients and steam briefly. Add the noodles.

3 Combine the cornflour, soy sauce, lemon juice and sugar in a small bowl. Add to the wok and simmer briefly to thicken. Serve garnished with chopped coriander or spring onion tops.

# Courgette Soup with Small Pasta Shells

*An attractive and refreshing soup which could be made using cucumber instead of courgettes.*

## INGREDIENTS

*Serves 4–6*

60ml/4 tbsp olive or sunflower oil

2 medium onions, finely chopped

1.5 litres/2$\frac{1}{2}$ pints/6$\frac{1}{4}$ cups chicken
   stock

900g/2lb courgettes

115g/4oz/1 cup small pasta for soup

fresh lemon juice

salt and pepper

30ml/2 tbsp chopped fresh chervil

soured cream, to serve

1 Heat the oil in a large saucepan and add the onions. Cover and cook gently for about 20 minutes until very soft but not coloured, stirring occasionally.

2 Add the chicken stock and bring to the boil.

3 Meanwhile grate the courgettes and stir into the boiling stock with the pasta. Turn down the heat and simmer for 15 minutes until the pasta is tender. Season to taste with lemon juice, salt and pepper.

4 Stir in the chervil and add a swirl of soured cream to serve.

# Chicken with Spiced Rice

*This is a good dish for entertaining. It can be prepared in advance and reheated in the oven. Serve with traditional curry accompaniments.*

### INGREDIENTS

*Serves 8*

900g/2lb boneless chicken thighs

60ml/4 tbsp olive oil

2 large onions, thinly sliced

1–2 green chillies, seeded and finely chopped

5ml/1 tsp grated fresh root ginger

1 garlic clove, crushed

15ml/1 tbsp hot curry powder

150ml/$^1$/4 pint/$^2$/3 cup chicken stock

150ml/$^1$/4 pint/$^2$/3 cup natural yogurt

30ml/2 tbsp chopped fresh coriander

salt and black pepper

*For the spiced rice*

450g/1lb/generous 2$^1$/4 cups basmati rice

2.5ml/$^1$/2 tsp garam masala

900ml/1$^1$/2 pints/3$^3$/4 cups chicken stock or water

50g/2oz/scant $^1$/2 cup raisins or sultanas

25g/1oz/$^1$/2 cup toasted chopped almonds

1 Put the basmati rice into a sieve and wash under cold running water to remove any starchy powder coating the grains. Then put into a bowl and cover with cold water and leave to soak for 30 minutes. The grains will absorb some water so that they will not stick together in a solid mass while cooking.

2 Preheat the oven to 160°C/325°F/Gas 3. Cut the chicken into cubes of approximately 2.5cm/1in. Heat 30ml/2 tbsp of the oil in a large flameproof casserole, add one onion and cook until softened. Add the finely chopped chillies, ginger, garlic and curry powder and continue cooking for a further 2 minutes, stirring from time to time.

3 Add the stock and seasoning, bring slowly to the boil. Add the chicken. Cover and cook in the oven for 20 minutes or until tender.

4 Remove from the oven and stir in the yogurt.

5 Meanwhile, heat the remaining oil in a flameproof casserole and cook the remaining onion gently until tender and lightly browned. Add the drained rice, garam masala and stock or water. Bring to the boil, cover and cook in the oven with the chicken for 20–35 minutes or until tender and all the stock has been absorbed.

6 To serve, stir the raisins or sultanas and toasted almonds into the rice. Spoon half the rice into a large deep serving dish, cover with the chicken and then the remaining rice. Sprinkle with chopped coriander to garnish.

# Cream of Spring Onion Soup

*A meltingly smooth soup of chicken stock, potato and spring onions.*

*Serves 4–6*

25g/1oz/2 tbsp butter

1 small onion, chopped

150g/5oz spring onions, white parts only, chopped

225g/8oz potato, peeled and chopped

600ml/1 pint/2$^{1}$/2 cups chicken stock

350ml/12fl oz/1$^{1}$/2 cups single cream

salt and white pepper

30ml/2 tbsp lemon juice

chopped spring onion greens or fresh chives, to garnish

1 Melt the butter in a saucepan and add all the onions. Cover and cook over very low heat for about 10 minutes or until soft.

2 Add the potatoes and the stock. Bring to the boil, cover again and simmer over a moderately low heat for 30 minutes. Cool slightly.

3 Purée the soup in a blender or in a food processor.

4 If serving the soup hot, pour it back into the pan. Add the cream and season. Reheat gently, stirring frequently. Stir in the lemon juice and garnish before serving.

# Hot Chicken Curry

*This curry has a delicious thick sauce with extra colour provided by chunks of red and green pepper.*

*Serves 4*

30ml/2 tbsp corn oil

1.5ml/$^1/_4$ tsp fenugreek seeds

1.5ml/$^1/_4$ tsp onion seeds

2 onions, chopped

2.5ml/$^1/_2$ tsp chopped garlic

2.5ml/$^1/_2$ tsp chopped fresh root ginger

5ml/1 tsp ground coriander

5ml/1 tsp chilli powder

5ml/1 tsp salt

400g/14oz can tomatoes

30ml/2 tbsp lemon juice

350g/12oz/2$^1/_2$ cups cubed chicken

30ml/2 tbsp chopped fresh coriander

3 green chillies, chopped

$^1/_2$ red pepper, cut into chunks

$^1/_2$ green pepper, cut into chunks

sprigs fresh coriander, to garnish

1 In a medium saucepan, heat the oil and fry the fenugreek and onion seeds until they turn a shade darker. Add the chopped onions, garlic and ginger and fry for about 5 minutes until the onions turn golden brown. Reduce the heat to very low.

2 Meanwhile, in a separate bowl, mix together the ground coriander, chilli powder, salt, tomatoes and lemon juice.

3 Pour this mixture into the saucepan with the onions and increase the heat to medium. Stir-fry for about 3 minutes.

4 Add the chicken pieces and stir-fry for 5–7 minutes.

5 Add the coriander, chillies and peppers. Lower the heat, cover and simmer for 10 minutes until the chicken is cooked.

6 Serve hot, garnished with fresh coriander sprigs.

## COOK'S TIP

For a milder version of this delicious curry, simply omit some or all of the green chillies.

# Chicken Vermicelli Soup with Egg Shreds

*This light soup can be put together in a matter of moments and is full of flavour.*

### INGREDIENTS

*Serves 4–6*

3 large eggs

30ml/2 tbsp chopped fresh coriander or parsley

1.5 litres/2$^1$/2 pints/6$^1$/4 cups good chicken stock or canned consommé

115g/4oz/1 cup dried vermicelli or angel hair pasta

115g/4oz cooked chicken breast, sliced

salt and pepper

1 First make the egg shreds. Whisk the eggs together in a small bowl and stir in the chopped coriander or parsley.

2 Heat a small non-stick frying pan and pour in 30–45ml/ 2–3 tbsp egg, swirling to cover the base evenly. Cook until set. Repeat until all the mixture is used up.

3 Roll each pancake up and slice thinly into shreds. Set aside.

4 Bring the stock to the boil and add the pasta, breaking it into short lengths. Cook for 3–5 minutes until the pasta is almost tender, then add the chicken, salt and pepper. Heat through for 2–3 minutes, then stir in the egg shreds. Serve immediately.

# Spicy Masala Chicken

*These chicken pieces are grilled and have a sweet-and-sour taste. They can be served cold with a salad and rice or hot with mashed potatoes.*

INGREDIENTS

*Serves 6*

12 chicken thighs
90ml/6 tbsp lemon juice
5ml/1 tsp chopped fresh root ginger
5ml/1 tsp chopped garlic
5ml/1 tsp crushed dried red chillies
5ml/1 tsp salt
5ml/1 tsp soft brown sugar
30ml/2 tbsp clear honey
30ml/2 tbsp chopped fresh coriander
1 green chilli, finely chopped
30ml/2 tbsp vegetable oil
fresh coriander sprigs, to garnish

1 Prick the chicken thighs with a fork, rinse, pat dry and set aside in a bowl.

2 In a large mixing bowl, make the marinade by mixing together the lemon juice, ginger, garlic, crushed dried red chillies, salt, sugar and honey.

3 Transfer the chicken thighs to the spice mixture and coat well. Set aside for about 45 minutes.

4 Preheat the grill to medium. Add the fresh coriander and chopped green chilli to the chicken thighs and place them in a flame-proof dish.

5 Pour any remaining marinade over the chicken and baste with the oil.

6 Grill the chicken thighs under the preheated grill for 15–20 minutes, turning and basting occasionally, until they are cooked through and browned.

7 Transfer the chicken to a serving dish and garnish with a few sprigs of fresh coriander.

# Chicken and Lentil Soup

*A chunky soup which will make a good lunchtime dish.*

INGREDIENTS

*Serves 4*

25g/1oz/2 tbsp butter or margarine

1 large carrot, chopped

1 onion, chopped

1 leek, white part only, chopped

1 celery stick, chopped

115g/4oz mushrooms, chopped

45ml/3 tbsp dry white wine

1 litre/1³/4 pints/4 cups chicken stock

10ml/2 tsp dried thyme

1 bay leaf

115g/4oz/¹/2 cup brown or green lentils

225g/8oz cooked chicken, diced

salt and black pepper

1 Melt the butter or margarine in a large saucepan. Add the carrot, onion, leek, celery and mushrooms. Cook for 3–5 minutes, until softened.

2 Stir in the wine and chicken stock. Bring to the boil and skim off any foam that rises to the surface. Add the thyme and bay leaf. Reduce the heat, cover, and simmer for 30 minutes.

3 Add the lentils and continue cooking, covered, for another 30–40 minutes, until they are just tender, stirring the soup from time to time.

4 Stir in the diced chicken and season to taste with salt and pepper. Cook until just heated through. Ladle the soup into bowls and serve hot.

# Tandoori Chicken

*A famous Indian/Pakistani chicken dish which is cooked in a clay oven called a tandoor, this is extremely popular in the West and appears on the majority of the restaurant menus. Though the authentic tandoori flavour is very difficult to achieve in conventional ovens, this version still makes a very tasty dish.*

## INGREDIENTS

*Serves 4*

4 chicken quarters

175ml/6fl oz/³/4 cup natural low-fat
    yogurt

5ml/1 tsp garam masala

5ml/1 tsp chopped fresh root ginger

5ml/1 tsp chopped garlic

7.5ml/1¹/2 tsp chilli powder

1.5ml/¹/4 tsp ground turmeric

5ml/1 tsp ground coriander

15ml/1 tbsp lemon juice

5ml/1 tsp salt

a few drops red food colouring

30ml/2 tbsp corn oil


*To garnish*

mixed salad leaves

lime wedges

1 tomato, quartered

1 Skin, rinse and pat dry the chicken quarters. Make 2 slits into the flesh of each piece, place in a dish and set aside.

2 Mix together the yogurt, garam masala, ginger, garlic, chilli powder, turmeric, ground coriander, lemon juice, salt, red food colouring and oil, and beat until well mixed together.

3 Cover the chicken quarters with the yogurt and spice mixture and leave to marinate for about 3 hours.

4 Preheat the oven to 240°C/475°F/Gas 9. Transfer the chicken pieces to an ovenproof dish.

5 Bake in the oven for 20–25 minutes, or until the chicken is cooked right through and browned on top.

6 Remove from the oven, transfer to a serving dish and garnish with the salad leaves, lime and tomato.

# SOUPS
# & STARTERS

# Chicken with Green Mango

*Green, unripe mango is used for cooking various dishes on the Indian sub-continent, including pickles, chutneys and some meat, chicken and vegetable dishes. This is a fairly simple chicken dish to prepare and is served with rice and dhal.*

### INGREDIENTS

*Serves 4*

1 green mango
450g/1lb/3$^1$/4 cups cubed chicken
1.5ml/$^1$/4 tsp onion seeds
5ml/1 tsp grated fresh root ginger
2.5ml/$^1$/2 tsp crushed garlic
5ml/1 tsp chilli powder
1.5ml/$^1$/4 tsp ground turmeric
5ml/1 tsp salt
5ml/1 tsp ground coriander
30ml/2 tbsp corn oil
2 onions, sliced
4 curry leaves
300ml/$^1$/2 pint/1$^1$/4 cups water
2 tomatoes, quartered
2 green chillies, chopped
30ml/2 tbsp chopped fresh coriander

1 To prepare the mango, peel, stone and slice the flesh thickly. Place the mango slices in a small bowl, cover and set aside.

2 Place the chicken cubes in a bowl and add the onion seeds, ginger, garlic, chilli powder, turmeric, salt and ground coriander. Mix the spices into the chicken and then add half the mango slices.

3 In a medium saucepan, heat the oil and fry the sliced onions until they turn golden brown. Add the curry leaves.

4 Gradually add the spiced chicken pieces and mango slices, stirring all the time.

5 Pour in the water, lower the heat and cook for about 12–15 minutes, stirring occasionally, until the chicken is cooked through and the water has been absorbed.

6 Add the remaining mango slices, the tomatoes, green chillies and fresh coriander and serve hot.

# Five Stuffings for Chicken

## BASIC HERB STUFFING

### INGREDIENTS

1 small onion, finely chopped

15g/$^1$/2oz/1 tbsp butter

115g/4oz/2 cups fresh breadcrumbs

15ml/1 tbsp chopped fresh parsley

5ml/1 tsp mixed dried herbs

1 egg, beaten

salt and black pepper

Cook the onion gently in the butter until tender. Allow to cool.

Add to the remaining ingredients and then mix thoroughly. Season well with salt and pepper.

### VARIATIONS

*Any of these ingredients may be added to the basic recipe to vary the flavour of the stuffing, depending on what you have in your store cupboard at home.*

1 celery stick, finely chopped

1 small eating apple, diced

50g/2oz/$^1$/2 cup chopped walnuts or almonds

25g/1oz/1 tbsp raisins or sultanas

50g/2oz/$^1$/4 cup chopped dried prunes or apricots

50g/2oz mushrooms, finely chopped

grated rind of $^1$/2 orange or lemon

50g/2oz/$^1$/2 cup pine nuts

2 rashers streaky bacon, chopped

## APRICOT AND ORANGE STUFFING

### INGREDIENTS

1 small onion, finely chopped

15g/$^1$/2 oz/1 tbsp butter

115g/4oz/2 cups fresh breadcrumbs

50g/2oz/$^1$/4 cup finely chopped dried apricots

grated rind of $^1$/2 orange

1 small egg, beaten

15ml/1 tbsp chopped fresh parsley

salt and black pepper

Heat the butter in a frying pan and cook the onion gently until tender.

Allow to cool slightly, and add to the rest of the ingredients. Mix until thoroughly combined and season with salt and pepper.

## RAISIN AND NUT STUFFING

### INGREDIENTS

115g/4oz/2 cups fresh breadcrumbs

50g/2oz/$^1$/3 cup raisins

50g/2oz/$^1$/2 cup walnuts, almonds, pistachios or pine nuts

15ml/1 tbsp chopped fresh parsley

5ml/1 tsp chopped mixed herbs

1 small egg, beaten

25g/1oz/2 tbsp melted butter

salt and black pepper

Mix all the ingredients together thoroughly. Season well with salt and pepper.

*Raisin and Nut Stuffing*

## PARSLEY, LEMON AND THYME STUFFING

### INGREDIENTS

115g/4oz/2 cups fresh breadcrumbs

25g/1oz/2 tbsp butter

15ml/1 tbsp chopped fresh parsley

2.5ml/$^1$/2 tsp dried thyme

grated rind of $^1$/4 lemon

1 rasher streaky bacon, chopped

1 small egg, beaten

salt and black pepper

Mix all the ingredients together to combine them thoroughly.

*Parsley, Lemon and Thyme Stuffing*

## SAUSAGEMEAT STUFFING

### INGREDIENTS

15g/$^1$/2 oz/1 tbsp butter

1 small onion, finely chopped

2 rashers streaky bacon, chopped

225g/8oz sausagemeat

2.5ml/$^1$/2 tsp mixed dried herbs

salt and black pepper

Heat the butter in a frying pan and cook the onion until tender. Add the bacon and cook for 5 minutes, then allow to cool.

Add to the remaining ingredients and mix thoroughly.

# Karahi Chicken with Mint

*For this tasty dish, the chicken is
first boiled before being quickly stir-
fried in a little oil.*

INGREDIENTS

*Serves 4*

275g/10oz chicken breast fillet, skinned
   and cut into strips

300ml/$^1$/$_2$ pint/1$^1$/$_4$ cups water

30ml/2 tbsp soya oil

2 bunches spring onions, roughly
   chopped

5ml/1 tsp grated fresh root ginger

5ml/1 tsp crushed dried red chilli

30ml/2 tbsp lemon juice

15ml/1 tbsp chopped fresh coriander

15ml/1 tbsp chopped fresh mint

3 tomatoes, seeded and roughly chopped

5ml/1 tsp salt

mint and coriander sprigs, to garnish

1 Put the chicken and water into
a saucepan, bring to the boil
and lower the heat to medium.
Cook for about 10 minutes or until
the water has evaporated and the
chicken is cooked. Remove from
the heat and set aside.

2 Heat the oil in a frying pan or
saucepan and stir-fry the
spring onions for about 2 minutes
until soft.

3 Add the boiled chicken strips
to the pan and stir-fry them
for about 3 minutes over a
medium heat.

4 Gradually add the ginger,
dried chilli, lemon juice, fresh
coriander, fresh mint, tomatoes
and salt and gently stir to blend all
the flavours together.

5 Transfer to a serving dish and
garnish with the fresh mint
and coriander sprigs.

# Poaching, Casseroling & Braising

## SIMPLE CHICKEN STOCK

*This all-purpose chicken stock may be used as the basis for a wonderful home-made soup.*

1 Put the giblets (the neck, gizzard and heart, but not the liver, as this makes stock bitter), or the carcass from a cooked chicken, into a pan and just cover with cold water.

2 Add a quartered onion, carrot, bouquet garni (bay leaf, thyme and parsley) and a few peppercorns. Bring to the boil, cover and simmer gently for 1–2 hours.

3 Remove any scum that rises to the surface with a slotted draining spoon. Alternatively, make the stock when you cook the chicken, by putting the giblets in the roasting tin around the chicken with the onion and herbs and just enough water to stop them from burning.

4 When the stock has set, carefully remove the fat from the surface with a spoon. Add salt to taste when using the stock.

## POACHING

*Poaching is a very gentle cooking method and produces stock for making a sauce afterwards.*

1 Put the chicken into a flameproof casserole with a bouquet garni (bay leaf, thyme and parsley), carrot and onion.

2 Cover with water and add salt and peppercorns. Bring to the boil, cover and simmer for about 1¹/₂ hours or until tender.

3 Cool in the liquid or lift out, shred, and combine with a white sauce.

## BRAISING

*This method can be used for whole chickens and pieces and is ideal for strongly-flavoured meat.*

1 Heat olive oil in a flameproof casserole and lightly fry a chicken or joints until golden.

2 Remove the chicken and fry 450g/1lb of diced vegetables (carrots, onions, celery and turnips), until soft.

3 Replace the chicken, cover tightly and cook very slowly on the hob or in a preheated oven at 160°C/325°F/Gas 3, until tender.

## CASSEROLING

*This slow-cooking method is good for large chicken joints with bones, or more mature meat.*

1 Heat olive oil in a flameproof casserole and brown the chicken joints.

2 Add some stock, wine or a mixture of both to a depth of 2.5cm/1in. Add seasonings and herbs, cover, and cook on the hob or in the oven as for braising for 1–1¹/₂ hours or until tender.

3 Add a selection of lightly-fried vegetables such as baby onions, mushrooms, carrots and small new potatoes about halfway through the cooking time.

# Moroccan Chicken Couscous

*A subtly spiced and fragrant dish
with a fruity sauce.*

*Serves 4*

15ml/1 tbsp butter

15ml/1 tbsp sunflower oil

4 chicken portions, about 175g/6oz each

2 onions, finely chopped

2 garlic cloves, crushed

2.5ml/$^1$/$_2$ tsp ground cinnamon

1.5ml/$^1$/$_4$ tsp ground ginger

1.5ml/$^1$/$_4$ tsp ground turmeric

30ml/2 tbsp orange juice

10ml/2 tsp clear honey

salt

fresh mint sprigs, to garnish

*For the couscous*

350g/12oz/2 cups couscous

5ml/1 tsp salt

10ml/2 tsp caster sugar

30ml/2 tbsp sunflower oil

2.5ml/$^1$/$_2$ tsp ground cinnamon

pinch of grated nutmeg

15ml/1 tbsp orange flower water

30ml/2 tbsp sultanas

50g/2oz/$^1$/$_2$ cup chopped blanched
 almonds

45ml/3 tbsp chopped pistachios

1 Heat the butter and oil in a
large pan and add the chicken
portions, skin-side down. Fry for
3–4 minutes, until the skin is
golden, then turn over.

2 Add the onions, garlic, spices
and a pinch of salt and pour
over the orange juice and
300ml/$^1$/$_2$ pint/1$^1$/$_4$ cups water.
Cover and bring to the boil, then
reduce the heat and simmer for
about 30 minutes.

3 Meanwhile, place the couscous
and salt in a bowl and cover
with 350ml/12fl oz/1$^1$/$_2$ cups water.
Stir once and leave to stand for 5
minutes. Add the caster sugar,
15ml/1 tbsp of the oil, the
cinnamon, nutmeg, orange flower
water and sultanas and mix well.

4 Heat the remaining 15ml/
1 tbsp of the oil in a pan and
lightly fry the almonds until
golden. Stir into the couscous with
the pistachios.

5 Line a steamer with greaseproof paper and spoon in the
couscous. Sit the steamer over the
chicken (or over a pan of boiling
water) and steam for 10 minutes.

6 Remove the steamer and keep
covered. Stir the honey into the
chicken liquid and boil rapidly for
3–4 minutes. Spoon the couscous
on to a warmed serving platter and
top with the chicken, with a little
of the sauce spooned over. Garnish
with fresh mint and serve with the
remaining sauce.

# Frying Chicken

Fried chicken is justifiably popular – crisp and brown outside and tender and juicy within. It's a quick and easy cooking method that can be applied to pieces of rabbit and hare and small turkey joints, too.

Dry the pieces thoroughly with kitchen paper before frying. If they are at all wet, they will not brown properly. If the recipe directs, lightly coat the pieces with egg and crumbs or with a batter.

---

### SUCCULENT FRIED CHICKEN

Mix 250ml/8fl oz/1 cup milk with 1 beaten egg in a shallow dish. On a sheet of greaseproof paper combine 150g/5oz/1¼ cups plain flour, 5ml/1 tsp paprika, and some salt and pepper. One at a time, dip eight chicken pieces in the egg mixture and turn them to coat all over. Then dip in the seasoned flour and shake off any excess. Deep-fry for 25–30 minutes, turning the pieces so they brown and cook evenly. Drain on kitchen paper and serve very hot. Serves 4.

---

1 To pan-fry, heat oil, a mixture of oil and butter, or clarified butter in a large, heavy-based frying pan over moderate heat. When very hot, add the chicken pieces, skin-side down.

3 To deep-fry, dip the pieces into a mixture of milk and beaten egg and coat lightly with seasoned flour. Allow coating to set for 20 minutes before frying. (Or dip them in batter just before frying.)

5 With a fish slice or tongs, lower the chicken pieces into the oil, a few at a time. Deep-fry, turning during cooking, until they are golden brown all over and cooked.

2 Fry until deep golden brown all over, turning the pieces during cooking. Fry until the pieces are thoroughly cooked. Remove pieces of breast before drumsticks and thighs. Drain on kitchen paper.

4 Half fill a deep pan with vegetable oil. Heat it to 185°C/365°F. You can test the temperature with a cube of bread; if it takes 50 seconds to brown, the oil is at the right temperature.

6 Drain on kitchen paper and serve hot. If you want to keep a batch of fried chicken hot whilst frying the rest, put it, uncovered, into a low oven.

# Chicken and Chorizo Tacos

*Use bought taco shells and fill with tasty minced chicken.*

*Serves 4*

15ml/1 tbsp vegetable oil

450g/1lb minced chicken

5ml/1 tsp salt

5ml/1 tsp ground cumin

12 taco shells

75g/3oz chorizo sausage, minced

3 spring onions, chopped

2 tomatoes, chopped

$^1$/2 head of lettuce, shredded

225g/8oz/2 cups grated Cheddar cheese

tomato salsa, to serve

1 Preheat the oven to 180°C/350°F/Gas 4.

2 Heat the oil in a non-stick frying pan. Add the chicken, salt and cumin and fry over a medium heat until the chicken is cooked through, 5–8 minutes. Stir frequently to prevent large lumps from forming.

3 Meanwhile, arrange the taco shells in one layer on a large baking sheet and heat in the oven for about 10 minutes, or according to the directions on the packet.

4 Add the chorizo and spring onions to the chicken and stir to mix. Cook until just warmed through, stirring occasionally.

5 To assemble each taco, place 1–2 spoonfuls of the chicken mixture in the base of a warmed taco shell. Top with a generous sprinkling of chopped tomato, shredded lettuce, and grated cheese.

6 Serve immediately, with tomato salsa to accompany.

# Making Poultry Sautés

A sauté combines frying and braising, producing particularly succulent results. It is a method suitable for pieces of poultry as well as for small whole birds such as quails and poussins.

As with frying, the poultry should be dried thoroughly with kitchen paper before cooking, to ensure that it browns quickly and evenly.

1 Heat a little oil, a mixture of oil and butter, or clarified butter in a heavy frying pan or sauté pan.

2 Add the poultry and fry over moderate heat until it is golden brown, turning to colour evenly.

3 Add any liquid and flavourings called for in the recipe. Bring to the boil, then cover and reduce the heat to moderately low. Continue cooking gently until the poultry is done, turning the pieces or birds over once or twice.

4 If the recipe instructs, remove the poultry from the pan and keep it warm while finishing the sauce. This can be as simple as boiling the cooking juices to reduce them or adding butter or cream for a richer result.

5 To thicken the cooking juices use equal weights of butter and flour mashed together. Use 25g/ 1oz of this "beurre manié" to 250ml/8fl oz/1 cup liquid. Add small pieces gradually to the hot juices and whisk until smooth.

6 Another method of thickening cooking juices is to use cornflour. Blend 10ml/2 tsp cornflour with 15ml/1 tbsp water and add to 250ml/8fl oz/1 cup juices. Boil, whisking, for 2–3 minutes, until the sauce is syrupy.

---

## COUNTRY CHICKEN SAUTE

Cook 175g/6oz chopped bacon in 10ml/2 tsp oil over a moderately high heat until lightly coloured. Remove and reserve. Dredge a 1.5kg/3$^{1}/_{2}$lb chicken, cut into eight pieces, in seasoned flour. Fry in the bacon fat until evenly browned. Add 45ml/3 tbsp dry white wine and 250ml/8fl oz/1 cup poultry stock. Bring to the boil and add 225g/8oz quartered mushrooms sautéed in 15ml/1 tbsp of butter and the reserved bacon. Cover and cook over low heat for 20–25 minutes, or until the chicken is tender.
Serves 4.

# Cajun Chicken

*Use cooked ham and prawns if you have them, but chicken and chorizo sausage are the main ingredients for this dish.*

INGREDIENTS

*Serves 4*

1.25kg/2$^{1}$/$_{2}$ lb fresh chicken

1$^{1}$/$_{2}$ onions

1 bay leaf

4 black peppercorns

1 parsley sprig

30ml/2 tbsp vegetable oil

2 garlic cloves, chopped

1 green pepper, seeded and chopped

1 celery stick, chopped

225g/8oz/1$^{1}$/$_{4}$ cups long grain rice

115g/4oz/1 cup chorizo sausage, sliced

115g/4oz/1 cup chopped, cooked ham

400g/14oz can chopped tomatoes with
   herbs

2.5ml/$^{1}$/$_{2}$ tsp hot chilli powder

2.5ml/$^{1}$/$_{2}$ tsp cumin seeds

2.5ml/$^{1}$/$_{2}$ tsp ground cumin

5ml/1 tsp dried thyme

115g/4oz/1 cup cooked, peeled prawns

dash of Tabasco sauce

chopped parsley, to garnish

1 Place the chicken in a large flameproof casserole and pour over 600ml/1 pint/2$^{1}$/$_{2}$ cups water. Add the half onion, the bay leaf, peppercorns and parsley and bring to the boil. Cover and simmer gently for about 1$^{1}$/$_{2}$ hours.

2 When the chicken is cooked lift it out of the stock, remove the skin and carcass and chop the meat. Strain the stock, leave to cool and reserve.

3 Chop the remaining onion and heat the oil in a large frying pan. Add the onion, garlic, green pepper and celery. Fry for about 5 minutes, then stir in the rice coating the grains with the oil. Add the sausage, ham and reserved chopped chicken and fry for a further 2–3 minutes, stirring frequently.

4 Pour in the tomatoes and 300ml/$^{1}$/$_{2}$ pint/1$^{1}$/$_{4}$ cups of the reserved stock and add the chilli, cumin and thyme. Bring to the boil, then cover and simmer gently for 20 minutes, or until the rice is tender and the liquid absorbed.

5 Stir in the prawns and Tabasco. Cook for a further 5 minutes, then season well and serve hot garnished with chopped parsley.

# Making Poultry Stock

A good home-made poultry stock is invaluable in the kitchen. It is simple and economical to make, and can be stored in the freezer for up to 6 months. If poultry giblets are available, add them (except the livers) with the wings.

### INGREDIENTS

*Makes about 2.5 litres/4 pints/10 cups*

1.12–1.35kg/2$^1$/2–3lb poultry wings, backs and necks (chicken, turkey, etc)

2 onions, unpeeled, quartered

4 litres/7 pints cold water

2 carrots, roughly chopped

2 celery stalks, with leaves if possible, roughly chopped

a small handful of fresh parsley

a few fresh thyme sprigs or

$^3$/4 tsp dried thyme

1 or 2 bay leaves

10 black peppercorns, lightly crushed

1 Combine the poultry wings, backs and necks and the onions in a stockpot. Cook over moderate heat until the poultry and onion pieces are lightly browned, stirring from time to time so they colour evenly.

2 Add the water and stir well to mix in the sediment on the bottom of the pot. Bring to the boil and skim off the impurities as they rise to the surface of the stock.

3 Add the remaining ingredients. Partially cover the stockpot and gently simmer the stock for about 3 hours.

4 Strain the stock into a bowl and leave to cool, then refrigerate.

---

### FRUGAL STOCK

❧

Stock can be made from the bones and carcasses of roasted poultry, cooked with vegetables and flavourings. Save the carcasses in a plastic bag in the freezer until you have three or four, then make stock. It may not have quite as rich a flavour as stock made from a whole bird or fresh wings, backs and necks, but it will still taste fresher and less salty than stock made from a commercial cube.

5 When cold, carefully remove the layer of fat that will have set on the surface.

---

### STOCK TIPS

❧

If wished, use a whole bird for making stock instead of wings, backs and necks. A boiling fowl, if available, will give wonderful flavour and provide meat to use in salads, sandwiches, soups and casseroles.

No salt is added to stock because as the stock reduces, the flavour becomes concentrated and saltiness increases. Add salt to dishes which contain the stock.

# Galveston Chicken

*An American favourite, crisp roasted chicken with garlic.*

INGREDIENTS

*Serves 4*

1.5kg/3–3$^{1}/_{2}$lb chicken

juice of 1 lemon

4 garlic cloves, crushed

15ml/1 tbsp cayenne pepper

15ml/1 tbsp paprika

15ml/1 tbsp dried oregano

2.5ml/$^{1}/_{2}$ tsp coarse black pepper

10ml/2 tsp olive oil

5ml/1 tsp salt

1 With a sharp knife or poultry shears, remove the backbone from the chicken. Turn it breast side up. With the heel of your hand, press down to break the breastbone, and open the chicken flat like a book. Insert a skewer through the chicken, at the thighs, to keep it flat during cooking.

2 Place the chicken in a shallow dish and pour over the lemon juice to coat.

3 In a small bowl, combine the garlic, cayenne, paprika, oregano, pepper and oil. Mix well. Rub evenly over the surface of the chicken.

4 Cover and let marinate 2–3 hours at room temperature, or chill overnight (return to room temperature before roasting).

5 Season the chicken with salt on both sides. Transfer it to a shallow roasting pan.

6 Put the pan in a cold oven and set the temperature to 200°C/400°F/Gas 6. Roast until the chicken is done, about 1 hour, turning occasionally and basting with the pan juices. To test, prick with a skewer: the juices that run out should be clear.

---

COOK'S TIP
❧

Roasting chicken in an oven that has not been preheated produces a particularly crispy skin.

---

# Spatchcocking Poultry

*Whole chickens, poussins, guinea fowl and game birds can be split in half and opened up flat like a book, to resemble the wings of a butterfly. They will then cook evenly under the grill or on a barbecue. A heavy chef's knife can be used to split the bird, but sturdy kitchen scissors or poultry shears are easier to handle.*

1 Set the bird breast down. Cut through the skin and rib cage along one side of the backbone, working from the tail end to the neck. Repeat on the other side of the backbone to cut it free. Keep the backbone for stock, if wished.

2 Turn the bird breast up. With the heel of your hand, press firmly on the breastbone to break it and flatten the breast.

## TESTING POULTRY
~

Overcooked poultry is dry, tough and tasteless, so knowing when a bird is done is crucial. The most reliable test for a whole bird is to insert a meat thermometer deep into the thigh meat (the internal temperature should be 79°C/175°F). Without a thermometer, you can test by piercing the thigh with a skewer or the tip of a knife; the juices that run out should be clear, not pink. Or lift the bird with a long two-pronged fork and tilt it so you can check the colour of the juices that run out of the cavity into the roasting tin. Pieces of poultry, particularly breasts, can be tested by pressing them with a finger; the meat should be firm but still slightly springy.

3 Fold the wing tips back behind the shoulders. Thread a long metal skewer through one wing and the top of the breast and out through the other wing.

4 Thread a second skewer through the thighs and bottom of the breast. These skewers will keep the bird flat during cooking, and will make it easy to turn over.

---

### GRILLING TIMES FOR POULTRY

*Note: Cook 10–15cm/4–6in from the heat; thinner pieces, less than 2.5cm/1in nearer the heat.*
*If the poultry seems to be browning too quickly, turn down the heat slightly.*

| | |
|---|---|
| POUSSIN, SPATCHCOCKED | 20–25 minutes |
| SPRING CHICKEN, SPLIT IN HALF OR SPATCHCOCKED | 25–30 minutes |
| ROASTING CHICKEN, SPLIT IN HALF OR SPATCHCOCKED | 30–40 minutes |
| CHICKEN BREAST, DRUMSTICK, THIGH | 30–35 minutes |
| SKINLESS BONELESS CHICKEN BREAST | 10–12 minutes |
| BONELESS DUCK BREAST | 10–12 minutes |

# Indian Spiced Chicken

*Tender marinated chicken pieces which can be served hot or cold.*

*Serves 4*

1.75kg/4–4¹/₂lb chicken

mixed salad leaves, e.g. frisée and oakleaf lettuce or radicchio, to serve

*For the marinade*

150ml/¹/₄ pint/²/₃ cup plain low-fat yogurt

5ml/1 tsp ground paprika

10ml/2 tsp grated fresh root ginger

1 garlic clove, crushed

10ml/2 tsp garam masala

2.5ml/¹/₂ tsp salt

red food colouring (optional)

juice of 1 lemon

1 Joint the chicken and divide it into 8 pieces, using a sharp knife.

2 Mix all the marinade ingredients in a large dish, add the chicken pieces to coat and chill for 4 hours or overnight to allow the flavours to penetrate the flesh.

3 Preheat the oven to 200°C/400°F/Gas 6. Remove the chicken pieces from the marinade and arrange them in a single layer in a large ovenproof dish. Bake for 30–40 minutes or until tender. Reserve the marinade.

4 Baste with a little of the marinade while cooking. Arrange on a bed of salad leaves and serve hot or cold.

# Boning a Chicken

*For the purpose of stuffing and to make carving simple, it is essential to bone a chicken. Use a sharp knife with a short blade. Work in short, scraping movements, keeping the knife against the bone at all times, to leave the carcass clean.*

*This is a fiddly job, so allow yourself plenty of time.*

*Save the chicken bones, which will be ideal for making chicken stock.*

1 Remove any trussing string. Cut off the wing tips (pinions) and discard. With a short-bladed, sharp knife cut the skin along the underside (backbone) of the chicken. Carefully work the skin and flesh away from the carcass with the knife until the leg joints are exposed.

2 Cut the sinew between the ball and socket joints. This sinew joins the thigh bones and wings to the carcass.

3 Holding the rib cage away from the chicken body, carefully scrape the breastbone clean and cut the carcass away from the skin. Take great care not to cut through the skin, or the stuffing will burst out of the hole.

4 Take hold of the thigh bone in one hand, and with the knife scrape the flesh down the bone to the next joint.

5 Cut around the joint and continue cleaning the drumstick until the whole leg bone is free. Repeat with the other leg and both the wings. Lay the chicken flat and turn the flesh of the legs and wings inside the chicken. Flatten the flesh neatly ready for stuffing.

---

### HANDLING RAW POULTRY

Raw poultry may harbour harmful organisms, such as salmonella bacteria, so it is vital to take care in its preparation. Always wash your hands, chopping board, knife and poultry shears in hot soapy water before and after handling poultry. If possible use a chopping board that can be washed at high temperature in a dishwasher and always keep a chopping board just for the preparation of raw poultry. Thaw frozen poultry completely before cooking.

# Chilli Chicken

*Serve as a simple supper dish with boiled potatoes and broccoli, or as a party dish with rice.*

INGREDIENTS

*Serves 4*

12 chicken thighs

15ml/1 tbsp olive oil

1 onion, thinly sliced

1 garlic clove, crushed

5ml/1 tsp chilli powder or 1 red chilli, chopped

400g/14oz can chopped tomatoes, with the juice

5ml/1 tsp caster sugar

425g/15oz can red kidney beans, drained

salt and black pepper

1 Cut the chicken into large cubes, removing all skin and bones. Heat the oil in a large flameproof casserole and brown the chicken pieces on all sides. Remove with a slotted spoon and keep warm.

2 Add the onion and garlic to the casserole and cook gently until soft. Stir in the chilli powder or chopped red chilli and cook for 2 minutes. Add the tomatoes with their juice, seasoning and sugar. Bring to the boil.

3 Replace the chicken pieces, cover the casserole and simmer for about 30 minutes until tender.

4 Add the red kidney beans and gently cook for a further 5 minutes to heat them through before serving.

# Jointing Poultry

Although chickens and other poultry are sold already jointed into halves, quarters, breasts, thighs and drumsticks, sometimes it makes sense to buy a whole bird and to do the job yourself. That way you can prepare four larger pieces or eight smaller ones, depending on the recipe, and you can cut the pieces so the backbone and other bony bits (which can be saved for stock) are not included. In addition, a whole bird is cheaper to buy than pieces.

A sharp knife and sturdy kitchen scissors or poultry shears make the job of jointing poultry very easy.

1 With the sharp knife, cut through the skin on one side of the body down to where the thigh joins the body. Bend the leg out away from the body and twist it to break the ball and socket joint.

2 Hold the leg out away from the body and cut through the ball and socket joint, taking the "oyster meat" from the backbone with the leg. Repeat on the other side.

3 To separate the breast from the back, cut through the flap of skin just below the rib cage, cutting towards the neck. Pull the breast and back apart, cutting through the joints that connect them. Reserve the back for stock.

4 Turn the whole breast over, skin side down. Take one side of the breast in each hand and bend back firmly so the breastbone pops free. Loosen the bone on both sides with your fingers and using a knife to help, remove it.

5 Cut the breast lengthways in half, cutting through the wishbone. You now have 2 breasts with wings attached and 2 leg portions.

6 For 8 pieces, cut each breast in half at an angle so that some breast is included with each wing. Trim off any protruding bones.

7 With the knife, cut each leg portion through the ball and socket joint to separate the thigh and drumstick.

### TERMS FOR CHICKEN BREASTS

If the wing is left attached to the chicken breast, this is termed a "supreme". If the breast is completely boned, it is called a "fillet".

# Chinese Chicken Wings

*These are best eaten with fingers as a starter. Make sure you provide finger bowls and plenty of paper napkins, it could get messy.*

*Serves 4*

12 chicken wings

3 garlic cloves, crushed

4cm/1½in piece fresh root ginger, grated

juice of 1 large lemon

45ml/3 tbsp soy sauce

45ml/3 tbsp clear honey

2.5ml/½ tsp chilli powder

150ml/¼ pint/⅔ cup chicken stock

salt and black pepper

lemon wedges, to garnish

3 Preheat the oven to 220°C/ 425°F/Gas 7. Remove the wings from the marinade and arrange in a single layer in a roasting tin. Bake for 20–25 minutes, basting at least twice with the marinade during cooking.

4 Place the wings on a serving plate. Add the stock to the marinade in the roasting tin, and bring to the boil. Cook to a syrupy consistency and spoon a little over the wings. Serve garnished with lemon wedges.

1 Remove the wing tips and use to make the stock. Cut the wings into two pieces.

2 Mix the remaining ingredients, apart from the stock, together and coat the chicken pieces in the mixture. Cover with clear film and marinate overnight.

# Roasting Poultry

*Where would family gatherings be without the time-honoured roast bird? But beyond the favourite chicken, all types of poultry can be roasted – from small poussins to large turkeys. However, older tougher birds are better pot-roasted.*

## SIMPLE ROAST CHICKEN

❧

Squeeze the juice from a halved lemon over a 1.35–1.5kg/ 3–3$^1$/$_2$lb chicken, then push the lemon halves into the body cavity. Smear 15g/$^1$/$_2$oz softened butter over the breast. Roast in a 190°C/375°F/Gas 5 oven for about 1$^1$/$_4$ hours. Skim all fat from the roasting juices, then add 120ml/4fl oz/$^1$/$_2$ cup water and bring to the boil, stirring well to mix in the browned bits. Season with salt and pepper, and serve this sauce with the chicken. Serves 4.

1 Wipe the bird inside and out with damp kitchen paper, stuff, if directed, and truss it. Spread the breast of chicken with soft butter or oil; bard a lean game bird; prick the skin of duck or goose.

2 Set the bird breast up on a rack in a small roasting tin or shallow baking dish. If you are roasting a lean game bird, set the bird in the tin breast down.

3 Roast the bird, basting every 10 minutes after the first 30 minutes with the juices and fat in the tin. Turn if directed. If browning too quickly, cover with foil.

4 Put the bird on a carving board and leave to rest for at least 15 minutes before serving. Meanwhile make a simple sauce or gravy with the juices in the tin.

## ROASTING TIMES FOR POULTRY

*Note: Cooking times given here are for unstuffed birds.*
*For stuffed birds, add 20 minutes to the total roasting time.*

| | | |
|---|---|---|
| POUSSIN | 450–700g/1–1$^1$/$_2$lb | 1–1$^1$/$_4$ hours at 180°C/350°F/Gas 4 |
| CHICKEN | 1.12–1.35kg/2$^1$/$_2$–3lb | 1–1$^1$/$_4$ hours at 190°C/375°F/Gas 5 |
| | 1.5–1.8kg/3$^1$/$_2$–4lb | 1$^1$/$_4$–2 hours at 190°C/375°F/Gas 5 |
| | 2.2–2.25kg/4$^1$/$_2$–5lb | 1$^1$/$_2$–2 hours at 190°C/375°F/Gas 5 |
| | 2.25–2.7kg/5–6lb | 1$^3$/$_4$–2$^1$/$_2$ hours at 190°C/375°F/Gas 5 |
| DUCK | 1.35–2.25kg/3–5lb | 1$^3$/$_4$–2$^1$/$_4$ hours at 200°C/400°F/Gas 6 |
| GOOSE | 3.6–4.5kg/8–10lb | 2$^1$/$_2$–3 hours at 180°C/350°F/Gas 4 |
| | 4.5–5.4kg/10–12lb | 3–3$^1$/$_2$ hours at 180°C/350°F/Gas 4 |
| TURKEY | 2.7–3.6kg/6–8lb | 3–3$^1$/$_2$ hours at 160°C/325°F/Gas 3 |
| *(whole bird)* | 3.6–5.4kg/8–12lb | 3–4 hours at 160°C/325°F/Gas 3 |
| | 5.4–7.2kg/12–16lb | 4–5 hours at 160°C/325°F/Gas 3 |
| TURKEY | 1.8–2.7kg/4–6lb | 1$^1$/$_2$–2$^1$/$_4$ hours at 160°C/325°F/Gas 3 |
| *(whole breast)* | 2.7–3.6kg/6–8lb | 2$^1$/$_4$–3$^1$/$_4$ hours at 160°C/325°F/Gas 3 |

## PROTECT & FLAVOUR

❧

Before roasting, loosen the skin on the breast by gently easing it away from the flesh with your fingers. Press in softened butter – mixed with herbs or garlic for extra flavour – and smooth back the skin. To bard poultry, cover the breast with slices of bacon before roasting.

# Spatchcocked Devilled Poussins

*"Spatchcock", perhaps a corruption of the old Irish phrase "despatch a cock", refers to birds that are split and skewered flat for cooking.*

### INGREDIENTS

Serves 4

15ml/1 tbsp English mustard powder

15ml/1 tbsp paprika

15ml/1 tbsp ground cumin

20ml/4 tsp tomato ketchup

15ml/1 tbsp lemon juice

65g/2$^{1}$/2oz/5 tbsp butter, melted

4 poussins, about 450g/1lb each

salt

1 Mix together the mustard, paprika, cumin, ketchup, lemon juice and salt until smooth, then gradually stir in the butter.

2 Using game shears or strong kitchen scissors, split each poussin along one side of the backbone, then cut down the other side of the backbone to remove it.

3 Open out a poussin, skin side uppermost, then press down firmly with the heel of your hand. Pass a long skewer through one leg and out through the other to secure the bird open and flat. Repeat with the remaining birds.

4 Spread the mustard mixture evenly over the skin of the birds. Cover loosely and leave in a cool place for at least 2 hours. Preheat the grill.

5 Place the birds, skin side up, under the grill and cook for about 12 minutes. Turn over, baste and cook for a further 7 minutes, until the juices run clear.

---

### COOK'S TIP

Spatchcocked poussins cook well on the barbecue. Make sure the coals are hot, then cook for 15–20 minutes, turning and basting frequently.

# Trussing Poultry

Trussing holds a bird together during cooking so that it keeps a neat, attractive shape. If the bird is stuffed, trussing prevents the stuffing falling out. You can truss with strong string or with poultry skewers.

An alternative to the method shown here is to use a long trussing needle and fine cotton string: make two passes, in alternate directions, through the body at the open end, from wing to wing, and tie. Then pass the needle through the parson's nose and tie the string around the ends of the drumsticks.

Remove trussing before serving.

1 For an unstuffed bird: set it breast down and pull the neck skin over the neck opening. Turn the bird breast up and fold each wing tip back, over the skin, to secure firmly behind the shoulder.

2 Press the legs firmly down and into the breast. If there is a band of skin across the parson's nose, fold back the ends of the drumsticks and tuck them under the skin.

3 Otherwise, cross the knuckle ends of the drumsticks or bring them tightly together. Loop a length of string several times around the drumstick ends, tie a knot and trim off excess string.

4 For a stuffed bird: fold the wing tips back as above. After stuffing the neck end, fold the flap of skin over the opening and secure it with a skewer, then fold over the wing tips.

5 Put any stuffing or flavourings (herbs, lemon halves, apple quarters and so on) in the body cavity, then secure the ends of the drumsticks as above, tying in the parson's nose, too.

6 Or, the cavity opening can be closed with skewers: insert two or more skewers across the opening, threading them through the skin several times.

7 Lace the skewers together with string. Tie the drumsticks together over the skewers.

## STUFFING TIPS

Only use stuffing that is cool, not hot or chilled. Pack it loosely in the bird and cook any leftovers separately. Stuff poultry just before cooking. Do not stuff the body cavity of a large bird because this could inhibit heat penetration, and thus harmful bacteria may not be destroyed.

# Chicken in Green Almond Sauce

*This casserole with its spicy sauce originates from Mexico.*

*Serves 6*

1.5kg/3–3$^1$/2lb chicken, cut into serving
    pieces
475ml/16fl oz/2 cups chicken stock
1 onion, chopped
1 garlic clove, chopped
115g/4oz/2 cups fresh coriander, coarsely
    chopped
1 green pepper, seeded and chopped
1 *jalapeño* chilli, seeded and chopped
275g/10oz can tomatillos (Mexican green
    tomatoes)
115g/4oz/1 cup ground almonds
30ml/2 tbsp corn oil
salt
fresh coriander sprig, to garnish
rice, to serve

1 Put the chicken pieces into a flameproof casserole or shallow pan. Pour in the stock, bring to a simmer, cover and cook for about 45 minutes, until tender. Drain the stock into a measuring jug and set aside.

2 Put the onion, garlic, coriander, green pepper, chilli, tomatillos with their juice and the almonds in a food processor. Purée fairly coarsely.

3 Heat the oil in a frying pan, add the almond mixture and cook over a low heat, stirring with a wooden spoon, for 3–4 minutes. Scrape into the casserole or pan with the chicken.

4 Make the stock up to 475ml/ 16fl oz/2 cups with water, if necessary. Stir it into the casserole or pan. Mix gently and simmer just long enough to blend the flavours and heat the chicken pieces through. Add salt to taste. Serve at once, garnished with coriander and accompanied by rice.

---

### COOK'S TIP

If the colour of the sauce seems a
little pale, add 2–3 outer leaves of
dark green cos lettuce. Cut out
the central veins, chop the leaves
and add at step 2.

---

# Cuts of Chicken

*Chicken pieces are available pre-packaged in various forms. If you do not want to buy a whole bird, you can make your choice from the many selected cuts on the market.*

*Some cooking methods are especially suited to specific cuts of poultry.*

**Liver**
This makes a wonderful addition to pâtés or to salads.

**Drumstick**
The drumstick is a firm favourite for barbecuing or frying, either in batter or rolled in breadcrumbs.

**Wing**
The wing does not supply much meat, and is often barbecued or fried.

**Skinless boneless thigh**
This makes tasks such as stuffing and rolling much quicker, as it is already skinned and jointed.

**Thigh**
The thigh is suitable for casseroling and other slow-cooking methods.

**Breast**
The tender white meat can be simply cooked in butter, or can be stuffed for extra flavour.

**Minced chicken**
This is not as strongly flavoured as, say, minced beef but it may be used as a substitute in some recipes.

**Leg**
This comprises the drumstick and thigh. Large pieces with bones, such as this, are suitable for slow-cooking, such as casseroling or poaching.

# Index

# Choosing a Chicken

*A fresh chicken should have a plump breast and the skin should be creamy in colour. The tip of the breast bone should be pliable.*

*A bird's dressed weight is taken after plucking and drawing and may include the giblets (neck, gizzard, heart and liver). A frozen chicken must be thawed slowly in the fridge or a cool room. Never put it in hot water, as this will toughen the flesh and is dangerous as it allows bacteria to multiply.*

**Poussins**
These are four to six weeks old and weigh 450g–550g/1–1$^1$/4lb. One is enough for one person.

**Double poussins**
These are eight to ten weeks old and weigh 800–900g/1$^3$/4–2lb. One will serve two people. Poussins are best roasted, grilled or pot-roasted.

**Boilers**
These are about twelve months and over and weigh between 2–3kg/4–6lb. They require long, slow cooking, around 2–3 hours, to make them tender.

**Roasters**
These birds are about six to twelve months old and weigh 1.5–2kg/3–4lb. One will feed a family.

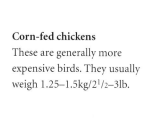

**Corn-fed chickens**
These are generally more expensive birds. They usually weigh 1.25–1.5kg/2$^1$/2–3lb.

**Spring chickens**
These birds are about three months old and weigh 900g–1.25kg/2–2$^1$/2lb. One will serve three to four people.

# Introduction

Chicken is popular with children and adults alike. It is versatile and economical, and can be cooked with a wide variety of ingredients and flavours. It is low in fat and quick to cook, with very little wastage.

Chicken can be bought in many forms: whole, quartered or jointed into thighs, drumsticks, breasts and wings, with or without bones and skin, which makes preparation very easy. Minced chicken can be found at some large supermarkets, but the skinned flesh can be minced quickly in a food processor. Although it is convenient to buy portions individually packed, it is expensive. It is much cheaper to buy a whole chicken and prepare it yourself and cheaper still to buy a frozen chicken and defrost it thoroughly before using. To get the best results from a frozen bird, allow it to thaw slowly in a cool place overnight or until completely defrosted. Many types of chicken are available, such as free-range and corn-fed (with yellow skin) and all are full of flavour. Some have added herbs and flavourings, and others are self-basting with either butter or olive oil injected into the flesh. This helps to keep the flesh succulent. Baby chickens are called poussins and can be bought to serve whole or halved depending on their size. In fact, chicken can be bought at any weight from 450g to 2.75kg (1lb to 6lb) to suit the size of your family.

The recipes in this book are mostly based on a family of four people, but they can be easily halved for two or doubled for eight. There are chapters on soups, salads and pies as well as one pot meals, midweek meals and hot and spicy dishes to provide you with a delicious chicken meal for every occasion.

To Try:
pg. 29 chicken Goujons
pg. 132 Grilled Chicken w/ pica
de Gallo salsa

# CONTENTS

~